MAIN
STREETS
&BACK
ROADS
of New England

Cover photo: Art Donahue
Cover design: Jane Sheppard
Text and layout design: Casey Shain
Photo credits: Art Donahue, pages 1, 29, 71, and 131
Production credits: see page 166, which is an extension of this copyright page.

The pictures accompanying each story are actual video stills from the televised
shows, which were brought into Adobe ® Photoshop® 5.5, color corrected,
and made printer-ready by the book's designer.

Library of Congress Cataloging-in-Publication Data

Main streets & back roads of New England: the best of Chronicle's award-
winning WCVB-TV series.
  p.cm.
      ISBN 0-7627-1221-X (PBK.); ISBN 0-7627-1268-6 (HARDCOVER)
      1. New England—Description and travel. 2. New England—History,
Local. 3. New England—Biography. 4. Interviews--New England. 5. Country
life—New England. I. Title: Main streets and back roads of New England. II.
Chronicle (Television program)

F10.M34 2001
974—dc21   2001033959

Manufactured in Korea
First Edition/Second Printing

All information is accurate as of press time. However, the authors and publisher
urge you to call ahead before visiting any of the sites listed.

MAIN STREETS & BACK ROADS
of New England

The Best of Chronicle's
Award-Winning WCVB-TV Series

Written by Susan Sloane, Chris Stirling, and the Chronicle staff

The Globe Pequot Press

Guilford, Connecticut

CONTENTS

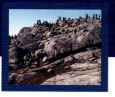  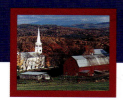 

ONLY IN NEW ENGLAND

ISLANDS & BYWAYS

CHRONICLE'S CHRONICLERS

Chronicle is many things. It is an exploration of the serious issues of the day. It is a portrait gallery of those who make life in New England so rich and interesting. It is a gentle meandering through the cities and villages of this unrivaled region of the country. What it is always is quintessentially New England.

Chronicle is also unprecedented in local television. Some have called it genius. That descriptive certainly applies to the program's heroic executive producer and managing editor, its distinguished anchors and reporters, its marvelously creative producers, and its amazingly gifted videographers and editors.

Chronicle is the pride of this television station and of its parent organizations, Hearst-Argyle Television and The Hearst Corporation.

Chronicle is, minimally, local television at its best and New England at its most glorious.

Paul La Camera,
President and General Manager, WCVB-TV

Viewers often ask me who are the most interesting people I've interviewed for Chronicle. They're curious about the movie stars and the famous political figures. But I tell them it's more often the Maine farmer who is not formally educated who knows more about the way the world works than the rest of us put together!

Movie stars and politicians are cautious; publicists and pollsters often dictate what they say. But country people are different: plain spoken and direct.

Much of their homespun wisdom has stayed with me for years. Dick Tracy (his real name), a farmer from Westhampton, Massachusetts, was gently chastising me for the way we busy city people rush around all day from one task to another, feeling tremendously self-important. He told me, "You know, the cemeteries are full of people who thought the world couldn't survive without them!"

May the characters and places you meet in this book linger with you, too, for years to come.

Mary Richardson,
Anchor

"You have the greatest job in the world," *Chronicle viewers often tell me.* How can I disagree? I've traveled the world, taken in wondrous sights, and interviewed fascinating people. And to think I get paid for such arduous duty!

But I'll let you in on a secret. We in New England live in one of the world's special places. For me, pointing my old Chevy along the back roads of Maine (with a videographer following behind) virtually guarantees that I'll stumble across an interesting story. And you thought we plan our trips?

The Chevy and I have explored remote fishing villages and offshore islands. We've motored from lakes to mountains, from Kittery in the south to the potato fields of Aroostook County hard by the Canadian border. I have lived a fantasy, chewing the fat with boat-builders, fishermen, poets, and game wardens. I learned early on that the venerable Maine writer John Gould was right when he told me, "Mainers are the friendliest people in the world, contrary to our image as stand-offish and cold."

I got to drive a fire engine in Jonesport, pilot an old steamboat on Moosehead Lake, take the controls of a train engine in

Brownville Junction, and skim the pines with an old bush pilot. I've been chased by a moose, chewed by black flies, and caught a few fish on company time. Who says this isn't a great country!

Peter Mehegan
Anchor

Chronicle's first program aired January 25, 1982. But it was a year and a half before our signature series, *Main Streets & Back Roads*, debuted in July of 1983, with an episode on Mystic, Connecticut.

The idea was to create a showcase for photography of New England's rural beauty, essays on the region's character and values, and profiles of the intriguing personalities who call this place home. Managing editor Judy Stoia wanted to title the series *Main Streets;* producer Charlie Kravetz wanted to call it *Back Roads.* They both got their way.

A successful *Main Streets & Back Roads* program combines heart, humor, and history, with a little homespun wisdom for good measure; it reminds us of the reasons why we choose to live in New England, despite the weather, the drivers, and the high cost of living.

I thank all of the talented reporters, producers, videographers, and editors who've created so many highlights in the last two decades. I hope these translations into print have done their work justice.

I dedicate this book to my wife Jane, my daughter Casey, and my son Kevin, and to my mother and father, who would have been proud to see it.

Chris Stirling
Chris Stirling
Executive Producer

Don't tell the boss, but mine is one of the easiest jobs in television. The most picturesque corner of the country is my canvas. Some of broadcasting's best videographers, producers, and editors are my colleagues. And our viewers are exceptional—with the intelligence and curiosity to appreciate depth and nuance in the New England character. It's truly a pleasure to bring a nightly portrait of New England to so discerning an audience.

Now we have the opportunity to double our fun. I never could have imagined that Chronicle would find its way to the printed page. Perhaps I should have been paying closer attention to Peter Mehegan's very first edition of "On the Road," and his conversation with Down East author John Gould.

"I made the crack one time that in Maine, we didn't write books, we lived them," Gould chuckled. "You went to your grange meetings, you went fishing, and you went out each fall after your deer. And finally, you *had* a book—you didn't *write* it. And when the pile was big enough, you sent it to a publisher."

That's just how it's been for us. Our main streets and back roads have led us here, to this book. Sit back and enjoy it—just as we've enjoyed collecting these stories over the past twenty years.

A special thank you to the cyber-savvy—Stephen, Rebecca and Joe—for their assistance and patience with their technically-challenged wife and mother.

Susan Sloane
Susan Sloane
Managing Editor

PEOPLE

GRANGE SOCIETY

A farmer's days are long. Nights can seem even longer. More than a century ago, America's farmers found a way to fill their quiet nighttime hours—with singing, dancing, and storytelling down at the local grange. A uniquely American social club, the grange developed a special stronghold up in Maine, where it clings to life to this day.

But in the age of HBO and MTV, can down-home humor and old-time music continue to thrive? We traveled to Maine in 1992 for an answer.

Greetings from the Grange

Long before television or radio, long before movies or electricity or the automobile, there was the Maine Grange. A fraternal order founded just after the Civil War in 1867, the Grange helped farmers across a healing nation cope with the desolate, hardscrabble existence of nineteenth-century rural life. The Grange brought culture, entertainment, and social support to people living in poverty and isolation.

Historian Stan Howe learned of the importance of the Grange in Maine by reading postcards, letters, and diaries from the 1800s. "The Grange brought all

The Grange has members in 37 states and the District of Columbia. It has many youth-oriented programs and promotes strong family values. The Grange holds a national convention each November, and even has a Web site: www.nationalgrange.org. While the Maine Grange has seen membership decline, it nevertheless maintains a state office in the capital of Augusta, with committees focusing on women's and youth activities.

kinds of joy to these very bleak lives," Howe says. "It had a literary program which involved skits and plays and meetings and music—all things that made these lives so much brighter, because these people were tremendously downtrodden in many ways and culturally deprived."

Today, of course, rural communities have many more entertainment and social options, but a hardy band of Maine Grangers continues to meet, keeping a fascinating slice of New England history alive.

A typical meeting may have 30 to 40 attendees, most aged 50 to 75. Entertainment might consist of banjo playing or a songfest

A Grange gathering, and Hazel Bean on piano.

of old favorites. One particularly talented grange member, Dot Canwell, plays the piano and whistles simultaneously. She's usually accompanied by a harmonica player.

The music gets the toes tapping, but it's the skits that get the big laughs. Skits include bits of cornball dialogue which reveal the understated, wry wit of Maine. For example:

MAN: "Tell me, Mrs. Songbird, have you ever been bedridden?"

MRS. SONGBIRD: "Oh my, yes. Hundreds of times here in the house. Two times out in the hayloft."

Or another:

MAN: "So, your wife picks out all your clothes."

OTHER MAN: "No she don't. She just goes along to tell me whether I like 'em or not."

Aroostook County is Maine's potato-farming country, and was once a hotbed of Grange activity. But the farming economy has faltered and Grange membership has dwindled.

On a tour of the Grange in Houlton, Maine, Kermit Esty demonstrates an old hand-crank Victrola, and talks about how things have changed. "The attendance isn't the same that it used to be. It has dropped off tremendously.

We recently lost a lady, Mabel White. She was chaplain of the Grange for over 30 years. She was an 80-year member, and she was 98 when she died. She was quite a gal."

Another longtime Grange member, Hazel Bean, has played piano at Grange meetings since she was a teenager. She sings an old song that laments the hardships of working the land:

> *Stay on the farm boys, stay on the farm,*
> *Though profits come in rather small.*
> *Stay on the farm boys, stay on the farm,*
> *Don't be in a hurry to go.*

Finishing her song, Hazel reflects on her long life, and the time she has left.

"I don't know what they'll do when I finally get my crown," she says. "They'll have to find somebody else to play. Hopefully there will be, somewhere along the line."

U P D A T E : You can still find Hazel at the piano whenever grange members meet. She's 89 years young, and playing just as she ever has. But one thing did change since our 1992 program: Hazel was married! She is now Hazel Bean Small. Sadly, her husband, Chester, recently passed away.

STORY *of a* STORYTELLER

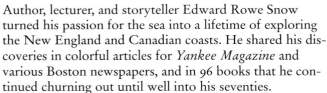

To generations of children, he was known as the Flying Santa. But Edward Rowe Snow's spirit for adventure wasn't limited to Christmas. Snow dug for buried treasure on Cape Cod, discovered wild horses on an island off Canada, and searched for pirate shipwrecks off New England's coast. In the winter of 1996—just months before his widow passed away—Chronicle recounted Snow's lifetime of adventure.

Author, lecturer, and storyteller Edward Rowe Snow turned his passion for the sea into a lifetime of exploring the New England and Canadian coasts. He shared his discoveries in colorful articles for *Yankee Magazine* and various Boston newspapers, and in 96 books that he continued churning out until well into his seventies.

Snow loved great stories and he relished telling them—the more bone-chilling, the better. His book titles included *Great Gales and Dire Disasters, Murder and Mutiny,* and *The Vengeful Sea.*

Snow led a group called the Boston Harbor Ramblers on weekly tours of the harbor islands. An old film clip of his tour commentary captures his fondness for the frightening: "And on Bird Island there is one delightfully gruesome story about the head of Captain Phillips, which was pickled."

Tom Smith, a former member of the Ramblers, remembers Mr. Snow well. "He was trying to take local history, which previously was dead and dull and black and white, and he was trying to colorize it. To make it popular and interesting," Smith recalls.

Coming from a long line of sea captains, Snow was born in the coastal community of Winthrop, Massachusetts in 1902. His thesis at Harvard was on the history of the Boston Harbor islands. His wife, Anna-Myrle Snow, swears she and Edward canoed to each of the 30 islands in the harbor.

Snow's daughter Dorothy tells of the time her dad was exploring Middle Brewster Island and came across a pile of rags wrapped around an old book. The book, dated 1637, was written in early Italian and was *bound in human skin.* He took the book home and found there were pinpricks over certain letters. The letters formed a code which spelled out a clue: *Gold is due east trees, Strong Island, Chatham outer bar.*

Dorothy recalls her father's reaction: "He was so excited he couldn't believe it. His brother had a metal detector and they went down there several times, and finally the metal detector went way off the charts. They started digging and they found a small treasure chest. Inside were a handful of coins. In all, they were worth a

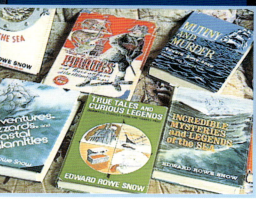

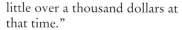
Anna-Myrle Snow

little over a thousand dollars at that time."

In his radio programs, Snow enthralled listeners with tales of shipwrecks and other astonishing legends of New England's maritime past. At lectures, he showed films of his adventures, including a trip to Sable Island off Canada, where the wild horses are believed to be descendants of horses that made it to shore after an 18th century shipwreck.

Snow also achieved fame as the Flying Santa. For 40 years, he would pack an airplane with gifts, put on a Santa suit, and fly over New England lighthouses to drop Christmas presents to the families of lighthouse keepers.

Snow kept in great physical condition all his life. When he was 62, he climbed Minot's Ledge Light off Cohasset, Massachusetts and dove 65 feet into the water, a spectacle captured on film. Anna-Myrle Snow states the obvious: "He was not afraid of anything."

Mr. Snow's old and deteriorating films were stored in his basement, and might have been lost forever. But Chronicle photographer Art Donahue, who produced this program, contacted Dorothy Snow and asked to see the films. With her permission, Donahue cleaned and restored the films.

Although Anna-Myrle Snow was in failing health, seeing all the great old footage of her late husband's life reinvigorated her in a way that surprised even her daughter Dorothy. On the spot, Mrs. Snow agreed to an interview and avidly described the remarkable experiences of her life with Edward. Two months later, she passed away.

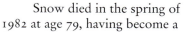

Snow died in the spring of 1982 at age 79, having become a legendary figure. His dedication to the Boston Harbor islands played a major role in preserving the islands for posterity. This strand of gems sprinkled across a newly cleaned Boston Harbor is now a national park.

Snow's contributions and exploits are remembered through an exhibit at the Lifesaving Museum in Hull. Each winter the museum sponsors the Snow Row, a boat race around the harbor islands in his memory. Baystate Cruises has named a tour boat after him.

In a fitting farewell, Anna-Myrle says her husband would always conclude his lectures with the same verse:

Farewell each
*   pretty little isle*
Farewell each
*   pretty shore*
May you be
*   blessed with*
*   Heaven's smile*
'Til time shall be
*   no more.*

STING OPERATION

In 1993, we discovered that an old staple of folk medicine was making a come-back. Bee sting therapy had again become the treatment of choice for a surprising number of New Englanders who suffer from arthritis, nagging sports injuries, and even multiple sclerosis. And, as we found out, foremost among its practitioners was a venerable old beekeeper and bee-liever in Vermont.

Charlie Mraz of Middlebury, Vermont has been a beekeeper all his life. "Ever since 1925, I've been a commercial beekeeper," Charlie says proudly, "keeping bees, producing honey, selling honey, and all that sort of thing." Even though Charlie is now 87 old and retired from the honey business, his bees are still in great demand. Actually, it's their stings that people want.

Charlie uses the stingers to treat arthritis and other diseases, though he began as a non-believer. "I started keeping bees when I was 14 years old, and back in the old days, beekeepers said bee stings were good for arthritis. Nonsense, I thought."

But a personal experience

Beekeeper Charlie Mraz

changed Charlie's mind. Back in 1934, as a last resort, he put a couple of honeybee stings into his arthritic knee. The next morning, he got out of bed. Something felt wrong. "I squat down, do a few knee bends," Charlie recalls. "I think for a minute. I have no more pain! That's what was wrong—I had absolutely no pain. Period."

Word spread fast, and over the years, Charlie found himself treating a host of maladies. "Lupus, scleroderma, all forms of arthritis, chronic pain, traumatic pain," he ticks off. "I can't remember them all." These days, Charlie finds there's always someone stopping by to get stung. "There isn't a day but what somebody comes," he

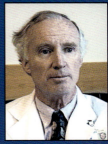

Mraz, left, and Dr. John Mills, above.

Mark Gratten, far right.

says. "Two or three . . . ten, twelve. This is all year 'round. It never stops."

Charlie is happy to help when he can. People stop by his house; some have an appointment, some don't. First, he talks to them to find out what's wrong. If he thinks he can help, he does a single sting to test for an allergic reaction. Those who pass get the full treatment. First comes the ice to numb the skin. Then, Charlie stings the problem area. The number of stings ranges from two or three to many more, depending on the severity and location of the pain.

"I just grab the bees by the head, then comes the sting," he explains. "The bee is very active, of course. Just touch it and it stings immediately. It takes hold in the skin, then I leave it in there for two or three minutes because the sting still works even after it goes in there—it keeps pulsing. Of course, the bee dies right away."

One of Charlie's "patients," Sue Barrows, winces as the stinger enters her skin. She's visiting for the first time, hoping that Charlie can help to relieve her multiple sclerosis. "The sting wasn't too bad," Barrows bravely reports. "Just a little jab. Not as bad as I thought it was going to

be." But this is only the first of many stings for Sue. "My sister and mother are bringing home a jar full of bees, so they're going to be at me with them—three times a week!"

A Stinging Endorsement

Because it's too soon for Sue to show any results, another of Charlie's believers shares his story. "I'm telling you, I was in so much pain," Mark Gratten begins. "Arthritis. I could just barely get around. Charlie gave me, I think it was six stings that first time I came up here." Gratten's patience paid off. "In about six months, about 1,900 bee stings later, I started feeling better—as far as the pain and stiffness," he recalls. "And around the ninth month, it was gone. I had no more arthritis. It was a miracle." It's tough to argue with success. "It's hard to believe that it works, but it does," Gratten insists. "No more bee stings for me—it's been three years and a couple of months."

It sounds convincing, but what do the professionals think? According to Dr. John Mills, who runs the Arthritis Clinic at Massachusetts General Hospital, there is indeed some theoretical background to bee sting therapy. "But the fact of the matter is that no controlled trial with bee venom

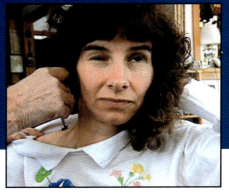

Patient Sue Barrows with Mraz.

has ever been conducted," Dr. Mills explains, and he points out that the chance of an allergic reaction, or even death, should be a concern to anyone considering bee sting therapy. As for the many success stories, he cautions, "In every trial of a new treatment for rheumatoid arthritis, some patients receive a placebo. And among those placebo patients, about twenty to forty percent get significant benefit." In other words, during drug testing, some arthritis sufferers report that plain old sugar pills have relieved their pain. The cure, says Dr. Mills, is in their heads.

Can the same be said for bee stings? One medical doctor, who asked that his name not be used, has been receiving stings for his multiple sclerosis and admits, "There's no question that there's a beneficial effect, especially in strength and mood. And there's no question in my mind that this has to be studied by the National Institutes of Health."

Charlie confirms there's interest in the traditional medical community. "We've got lots of doctors working with bee venom now, actually using it. But they keep quiet. They don't let anybody know they're doing it," he says.

Charlie also points out that venom therapy is nothing new. "This bee thing has been here for thousands of years. Even the ancients knew about it!" he says. And he has a theory about who first made the discovery: "I think the first caveman that robbed a beehive—if he had arthritis—found out he got better after he got the hell stung out of him."

So, to bee or not to bee? Charlie has a straightforward answer. "You don't believe it? You don't agree with it? It's O.K. with me. Suffer—I don't give a damn."

UPDATE: Charlie Mraz passed away in September of 2000, at the age of 94. With him went the art and science of bee sting therapy in Middlebury. Today, Mraz's son, Bill, runs the family business, Champlain Valley Apiaries. Along with honey and beeswax, Bill sells bee venom to laboratories, but he has decided against treating patients as his father did.

Meanwhile, researchers at Georgetown University Medical Center are conducting one of the first controlled studies on bee venom and pain relief. They are looking into the effects of bee venom on patients with multiple sclerosis, and expect to release findings by 2002.

CAPE ANN ARTISTS

Cape Ann stretches off the North Shore of Boston through parts of Gloucester, Rockport, Essex, Magnolia, and Manchester-by-the-Sea. Its coastal beauty has historically inspired artists and its harbors sustained fishermen. A recently discovered 19th-century masterpiece by the Cape Ann artist Fitz Hugh Lane brought us to the area in the spring of 1997.

The painting hung in the attic of a family home for decades, shrouded in darkness and encrusted in dirt. Then the owners called Boston's Skinner Auction House, asking for someone to evaluate a collection of furniture, ceramics, and paintings. Appraiser Sandy Niles remembers the day she walked in and saw the painting: "My gut was telling me it was a Fitz Hugh Lane, but my mind was telling me it couldn't be."

Sandy's first impressions were correct. The painting was indeed a Lane, from 1863, capturing the seascape off West Beach in Beverly. Lane's most recently auctioned painting had fetched a record $3.3 million; Skinner appraisers expected this find would bring even more.

First known as a lithographer in the 1830s, Fitz Hugh Lane was the most important American maritime painter before Winslow Homer. He was regarded as a leading artist in the luminist movement, producing a series of harbor scenes of New York and Baltimore. But his favorite locales were Boston and Gloucester, where he spent most of his 61 years in a waterfront home.

Courtesy: Cape Ann Historical Society

Fitz Hugh Lane

Gloucester Grows Up

Lane would hardly recognize the Gloucester of today, which has added tourists to its maritime mix, and traffic to its daily stresses, especially in summer. For proof, just try crossing Blynman Bridge—chances are, you'll wait . . . and wait. It is the busiest drawbridge on the Northeast coast, averaging about 7,500 openings a year with more than 20,000 vessels passing through.

Drawbridge operator Ron Kane doesn't have an easy job. "Every time we open the bridge someone gets angry," Kane says. In fact, Kane has even experienced cases of bridge rage. "They verbally express themselves or use physical gestures,"

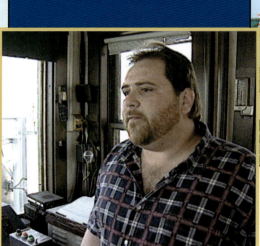

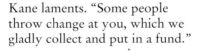
Drawbridge operator
Ron Kane, center.

Kane laments. "Some people throw change at you, which we gladly collect and put in a fund."

Art out of Adversity

One Gloucester resident we met seems unlikely to get upset over traffic jams. Artist Jon Sarkin is too busy creating art in his downtown Gloucester studio, making collages, multimedia constructions, and colored penciled drawings. The subjects: Cadillacs, cacti, aliens, and other non-Fitz Hugh Lane themes. "My stuff is not the Motif Number 1, seagull, fishy type of stuff," Sarkin acknowledges dryly.

And the route he took to his artistic calling was not the usual museum school, starving artist, gallery-showing path. Although he loved to draw as a child, Sarkin pursued a career as a chiropractor. And, until October of 1988, he was a successful one. But that month, while playing golf, he felt what he remembers as an explosion in his head. Sarkin developed tinnitus, a constant severe ringing in the ear. After a year of internal torment, he tried surgery to correct it.

"I was desperate because of the ringing, so I said, 'Let's go ahead,'" he recalls. The operation stopped the ringing, but shortly afterwards, Sarkin suffered a stroke and fell into a three-month coma. When he emerged, he was deaf in one ear, had permanent blurred vision, and walked with a limp. His chiropractic career was over. But the stroke had unleashed a pent-up reservoir of images and obsessions. His career as an artist had begun.

"I never thought at age 43 I would be this happy," Sarkin says. "It's ironic that you are privy to insights only through tremendous adversity."

The world may soon hear more about Jon Sarkin. When we visited him, he couldn't help sharing his big news: "Tom Cruise's film company has bought the rights to a stroke victim's story—that's me!" he exclaimed.

A life threatening scare. A total career makeover. Plans to put his life story up on the silver screen. Jon Sarkin has made the most of his second chance. And he's not done yet.

"I want my epitaph to read 'WOW! This guy really

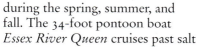

Beauport, above, and artist Jon Sarkin, center.

lived," he declares. "I hung on the surfboard of life, that's how I look at it."

Celebrating the Cape's Bounty

We don't know if Henry Sleeper ever hung ten. But he shared a passion for creativity with Fitz Hugh Lane, Jon Sarkin, and the other artists who've called Cape Ann home. Sleeper was an interior designer who decorated the homes of New England's elite, as well as the Hollywood digs of stars Joan Crawford and Fredric March. His own house—Beauport—began life as a seaside cottage on Gloucester's Eastern Point. From 1907 to 1934, Sleeper continually added to the structure until it was a sprawling mansion of 40 rooms, with every nook and cranny filled with a collection of objects. Beauport is now owned by the Society for the Preservation of New England Antiquities and open to the public.

So why do so many artists find Cape Ann a wellspring of inspiration? You can find out for yourself. Essex River Cruises, (800–748–3706) offers daily 90-minute tours during the spring, summer, and fall. The 34-foot pontoon boat *Essex River Queen* cruises past salt marshes, dolphins rare birds, and even the remnants of a movie set on Hog Island, the main filming location for *The Crucible.*

UPDATE: Can you put a price on natural beauty of the canvas kind? Skinner, Inc. found out on May 9, 1997. That's when the Fitz Hugh Lane from the attic—*View of West Beach, Beverly, Massachusetts, Sunset*—went on auction. The bidding started at $500,000 and escalated rapidly from there. At the end, two bidders, competing by phone, were left standing. The winner took the prize for $3.5 million, which at that time was the highest price ever fetched by an auction house outside of New York City. When the news broke, New Englanders everywhere rushed to their attics to make sure they hadn't overlooked anything.

The NUT LADY

She's been a guest on Good Morning America *and entertained* Howard Stern's *radio audience. She's been interviewed by* CBS This Morning *and featured on* Talk Soup. *But long before she became a media darling—back in 1984—Chronicle discovered Elizabeth Tashjian and her nut museum.*

Walking up the driveway of this elegant 12-room Victorian in Old Lyme, Connecticut, you get a slight hint that you're about to encounter something out of the ordinary. From beneath a stately chestnut tree comes the voice of an elderly woman. "Here's one that has already opened," the voice is saying. "When it gets very dry, it opens of its own accord." There is a sense of joy and marvel in the voice. Elizabeth Tashjian has just found a nut. It may seem like an ordinary nut, but for Tashjian, it is a thing of wonder.

Tashjian is conducting one of the regularly scheduled nutting expeditions she holds at her nut museum. On the day Chronicle visited, her audience was made up of students from the Old Lyme Middle School, who came to learn firsthand about the importance of nuts.

Wrapped in her signature silky purple cape, Tashjian commands the attention of her novice nutters. "Nuts have a heart," she'll tell anyone who'll listen. "Hard and prickly sometimes on the outside, but soft and sweet on the inside. That's my philosophy." She has even written an ode to the object of her heart's desire:

"Oh, nobody ever thinks about nuts.
Nuts can be so beautiful, if looked 'aright.
Take nuts home and handle them properly, artistically.
And feel a new taste being born."

Clearly, the visiting students are gaining knowledge no book can hold. "Nuts grew in the Garden of Eden," Tashjian tells them. "They've been nourishing mankind ever since creation began. Nuts are fresh tokens of primeval existence."

Since 1972, Tashjian has devoted the first floor of her home to the nut museum, and filled it to overflowing with nut art, jewelry, furniture, sculpture, and history. Displaying the lonely half of a pair of nut earrings, she asks visitors to be on the lookout: "If you should see a squirrel wearing an earring, you'll know it's the mate of this one."

According to Tashjian, her museum displays 185 varieties of nuts. (We declined her offer to count for ourselves.) Strolling past one of her massive framed paintings, she explains that her fascination with nuts began years ago, when she was a student at the National Academy of

Elizabeth Tashjian and her home-cum-museum, including the provocative cocoa-de-mer.

Design in New York City.

"Nuts have been speaking to me for a long time," Tashjian says. "Our family liked nuts. We had bowls and bowls of nuts. Nuts to eat, nuts to play with, and one day they became more than edible delights. A painting subject! Suddenly I decided well, I'm an artist, I'd like to alert people to the beauty of nuts, and I'm going to open a nut museum."

Nut Again

Because we couldn't get enough of Elizabeth Tashjian, we stopped in for a second visit in 1995. She stood by the door waiting for us, dressed in her memorable purple cape. It was as if we'd never left—except for the many, many additions to her collection. Pausing at a massive, 35-pound cocoa-de-mer, she states the obvious: "It looks . . . well, human. Very much like the human anatomy. I'm challenging Darwin's theory of evolution on this nut. I'm saying out with apes, and in with nuts. A joke at the material origin of man."

Tashjian's museum continues to evolve. Some of the newer artwork seems to carry a New Age message of harmony and cooperation, such as a painting that depicts nutcrackers surrounded by floating nuts. "In the outside world, nutcrackers are the nuts' mortal enemy," she explains. "Here, nuts and nutcrackers can be friends."

Tashjian insists she has no objections to her nickname. "They call me the nut lady. And if they call me that, I've taken the demerit mark off nuts," she states proudly. "When a young lad of eight presented me with a picture of his face pasted in a nutshell, I said 'Mission Accomplished!'"

UPDATE: The Nut Museum is still open, by appointment. Call ahead at 860–434–7636. Admission includes a small monetary fee—*and* one nut. Preferably, the kind you buy in the store. "I think that I have made America nut-conscious," Tashjian concludes, "and we're out to start a new era. A nut era."

MENTAL MAGELLANS

The village of Danville, Vermont, looks like many other small towns across New England, with its sugar maple trees, classic white church, and well-stocked general store. But if you pick the right week to visit, you'll find that Danville resembles no other town on this—or any other—planet. Chronicle's Andria Hall was on hand for 1992's annual convention of the American Society of Dowsers.

WELCOME ASD TO DANVILLE HOME OF THE DOWSERS

The scene is confusing, yet compelling. It is a sunny spring morning. Across the lawn, grown men move every which way as if in a trance. Their steps are slow. Their eyes are trained on strange-looking devices. Their hands hold these devices as carefully as they might carry the Holy Grail. These are dowsers—practitioners of the ancient art of locating underground water through the use of divining rods.

"Where's the water dome?" chants one believer. "Where's the water dome?"

"Turn this thing over," an instructor laughs as he adjusts an upside-down Y rod in a novice's hands. "Now you ought to be able to catch it!"

Dowsers believe that water draws a response from their chosen instruments, be it a forked branch, a pair of bent wires, or a pendulum. The four-day convention is a sort of harmonic convergence of like-minded mental Magellans, exploring the farthest reaches of the mind's capabilities.

Greg Storozuk teaches a course in basic dowsing. "I thought it was the biggest bunch of bull I'd ever heard of in my life," he admits, "until I ended up trying it." Storozuk was hooked fast. Recently, he packed up his rods and moved to Massachusetts from Colorado, where he did six years of dowsing for oil and mineral companies. By now, he must be itching for a real challenge, because he agrees to give Andria a quick lesson.

He instructs her in the proper handling of her metal L rods. Now comes the test. "What we're going to do is to stand back to back," Storozuk coaches. "You'll begin walking in this direction

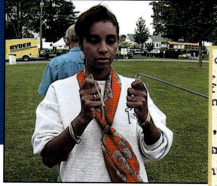

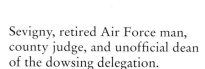

Andria Hall, left, Paul Sevigny's notes, center, and an avid dowser.

here, thinking only in your mind of a vein of underground, flowing water." Andria is told to concentrate on water until her rods show a response. Storozuk expects to get a telepathic response at the same time. They try the experiment several times, with various hits and misses. Toward the end, though, they hit what Andria describes as a "dowsing groove." When her rods shift downward, she is jubilant, and gleefully shouts, "Not bad for a novice, huh?"

A Long, Strong Tradition

Dowsing is no recently minted New Age fad. Dowsers have been depicted throughout the ages, showing up in ancient Chinese artwork and on murals inside Egyptian pyramids. Thomas Edison theorized that dowsing was connected to—no surprise here—electricity. Einstein weighed in with a vote for electromagnetism. Even the U.S. Marines got in on the act, dowsing for Vietnamese tunnels in the late 1960s. But no one *really* knows how—or if—it works.

"I think it's an ESP kind of thing," theorizes Paul Sevigny, retired Air Force man, county judge, and unofficial dean of the dowsing delegation. "Last Sunday I did my 2,650th well. Took me about five minutes."

But who's counting? Well, actually, Sevigny is. He has every one of his hits recorded in a book and turns the pages for our perusal. "This here was dowsing for the town of Waterbury. Got them a million gallons a day."

Dowsing goes far deeper than drilling wells. Sevigny has dowsed for just about anything people can't find on their own. He's even done some interstate dowsing, using just a map and his trusty Y rod.

"I had a priest from Maine call me one day in January and he said some good friends of his had lost a very valuable diamond ring," Sevigny recollects. "He wanted to know if I could help them. So I had them send me a diagram of the property, with the house located on it. This was the end of January. And I told them the ring was four feet from the end of the porch, under some bushes, and they'd find it in March when the snow went off." Sevigny pauses for the finale: "The 17th day of

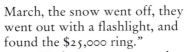

*Pros Storozuk, above,
and Paul Sevigny, far right.*

March, the snow went off, they went out with a flashlight, and found the $25,000 ring."

We don't want to say that we doubt Sevigny's account. But we spot a notation for the story in his record book and, unbeknownst to him, we make a call. Joanne Guillemette answers the phone. "It's true! I would have never believed it. My husband is a physician and we were saying, 'Yeah, right—get a life.' But we were so depressed we'd try anything," Guillemette recalls. "I thought I'd lost the ring downtown at my husband's office. But we found it months later under that bush."

Want to Give Dowsing a Try?

There are plenty of books available on the subject, and thorough instructions are offered on a number of Web sites. Or, you can dive deep into dowsing with a visit to the annual convention, usually held in mid-June.

Call the American Society of Dowsers for more information at 802–684–3417 or check out the society's Web site at http://dowsers.new-hampshire.net.

Dowsers have been holding their annual convention in Danville since 1958. What started as a group of 50 has grown to about 1,000 devoted diviners. Despite the crowds, Danville residents seem to take the annual invasion in stride. Some invite the odd dowser—or two or three—into their homes. "I have three in the house and two pitched in a tent out under a tree," Danvillian Gerry Buss says. "I think it's fun, and I think it's interesting!"

If there's a lesson to be learned in Danville during dowser week, perhaps it is this: spare the rod and spoil the fun.

The KNACKERMAN

At the height of leaf-peeping season, tourists come by the thousands to Woodstock, Vermont, for a slice—make that a sliver—of old New England. The village of Woodstock is quaint and pictur-esque, but hardly rustic. For tourists, the centerpiece is the Woodstock Inn and Resort, owned by Laurence Rockefeller. It is not the kind of place where you will find native Vermonters like Sy Osmer. In fact, you won't find many native Vermonters like Sy Osmer anywhere in the state. Peter Mehegan met up with Sy back in 1989.

Sy Osmer lives, not at all quietly, in the backwoods of Woodstock with his seven hunting dogs. He's 83 years old, but still works at his lifelong occupation. Osmer is a knackerman. He buys old and dead livestock and renders the meat and hides for sale. Before Peter paid a visit to Sy, he spoke with a few neighbors.

"Sy Osmer? He fulfills an important function," one local declares. "You know, cows don't live forever. When-ever an animal dies you call Sy. I put a call in and Sy was right around the next day."

A second neighbor chimes in. "He gives a dollar for a calf, usually ten dollars for a cow or horse or whatever. Then he renders it into dog food or hides and I guess some parts of it goes off to fertilizer," he explains. "I have a feeling when Sy stops doing what he's doing we are going to have to dig a lot of holes."

Bare-Bones Business

It's not hard to spot the knackerman himself on an approach to the Osmer place. He is dressed in a brown coat, held together by a single safety pin measuring at least three inches across. Atop his head sits something that was once a black hat; now it looks neither black nor much like a hat at all. Beneath the ex-hat is Sy's face, furrowed with more lines than Vermont has dirt roads.

The knackerman is happy to rehash his history. In what he calls "the good old days," Sy says he would have as many as five or six cows a day. But with the demise of so many dairy farms, business has tapered off. "Farmers keep going out of business," Sy sighs. "There's one just gone out of business right here in Union Village. He'd been at it for years—big herd of Holsteins."

Walking around to the side of the barn, Peter turns the corner and runs right into Sy's "merchandise." The collection of skeletons includes three or four cows plus a horse or two.

Sy laments that his way of life is disappearing. Who's to blame? "City people who bring their ideas up here with

Woodstock, Sy's grandfather's obituary, and Sy's old home.

'em, and drive all the regular poor people right out," Sy expounds.

Indeed, Sy has seen profound changes in Woodstock in his 83 years. "When I was a little fella, when I first got around the village, Woodstock had hitching posts right on the street," he recalls. "It was hard work to find a hitching post that wasn't already being used, to hitch a horse." But back then, horses were the only way to get around. "No cars at all back in those days," Sy says. "People said cars would have to be outlawed because they scared the horses and killed people. Now the cars are here, and the driving horse is gone."

Outside the barn door, Peter watches as Sy skins a raccoon, mesmerized by the knackerman's swift and steady hand. When asked what kind of knife he likes to use, Sy replies, "This is what they call a skinning knife," and offers no further explanation.

Happy Hunting Grounds

Sy is an independent sort—a lifelong bachelor, content to live in his solitary manner without so much as a telephone. Just like his neighbors, Laurence and Mary Rockefeller, he is determined to hold on to his piece of Vermont.

Peter asks if Sy knows Laurence Rockefeller personally. "Nope, can't say I ever met him," he responds.

"He hasn't come down to say hello?" Peter pushes, with a grin.

"Oh no, he's got a big farm here in Woodstock, and once in a while I get an animal."

Peter won't let go. "But he's never come down for coffee or anything like that?"

"No, I don't think he's seen too much."

Having had his fun at the Rockefellers' expense (they can afford it, after all), Peter moves on and asks Sy about his magnificent spread of pasture and woodlands—300 acres in all—wondering if developers have ever tried to scoop it up. Sy doesn't mince words: "There was a fellow down here in the spring and I told him right off the bat. I said, 'You are wasting your time and mine too.'"

"So you send them on their way?"

"Yeah, I just tell them I am not interested."

"And you are not tempted by all that money you could make, Sy?"

"No. The government would take a third of it anyway, if not more, in taxes. And besides, a man needs a place to go hunting."

End of subject.

A Page from the Past

Until 20 years ago, Sy lived in the house where he was

born—a house never equipped with electricity. Today, it is a tumbled-down ruin. Stepping gingerly inside, Peter makes a discovery amid a jumble of family memorabilia scattered on the floor: a copy of the *Vermont Standard* from January 23, 1913. Scanning the headlines on the fragile yellowed page, Peter asks, "There's the death of somebody here. Would this be your dad? William Alfred Osmer. And here's a photo."

"No, that would be my grandfather. It probably talks about his racehorsing—he used to have racehorses."

"No," Peter counters, "it's his obituary. Right here on page one. Well I'll be darned, he was only 54 when he died."

Sy makes his way across the room to take a look. Despite Peter's excitement, Sy appears indifferent.

"He had tuberculosis. In those days you got tuberculosis, you were a dead man. There was no cure for it. That was very common too."

"Here," Peter says, handing Sy the newspaper, "take that."

"Yeah, I'll take that." Not convinced that Sy understands what's just been placed in his hands, Peter adds, "That's something. Your grandfather right there on page one."

"That's right, that's him," Sy says. "There used to be a big picture hung up here, then somebody stole it. But now I can go to work and have another one made—this is the only picture of him that I know of. You done me a favor. I'll put that right into a safe and just as soon as I have a bit of time, I'll have another picture made."

UPDATE: There are no knackermen left in Woodstock; Sy passed away a few years after Peter's visit. His 300 acres are now in the hands of others—two wealthy out-of-staters who've "buried and bulldozed" the land, neighbor Dick Catlin reports. "They've reshaped everything—there are big, huge lawns where his woods were. It looks more like Wellesley Hills than Woodstock. If Sy could come back, he just wouldn't get it—he wouldn't get it at all."

The MILKMAN

Do you remember? Glass bottles topped by paper caps. The comfort and dependability of daily deliveries. A neatly pressed uniform and a smile, no matter the weather or the size of the bill.

Back in 1986, Chronicle wondered whether New Englanders still had need for the local milkman. We got our answer—and much more—from Maine's Cliff Plourd.

The alarm clock rings. It's 4:30 in the morning. Sunrise won't come to Maine for two hours yet, but Cliff Plourd is up, out, and on the road. He's seated behind the ice-crusted windshield of his 15-year-old truck. The temperature stands at ten below, and the winds whip through holes in the floorboards. But it's not the weather that bothers him. It's the thought of another breakdown. He's had his share of them.

Nevertheless, just like those postal workers, Cliff must make his appointed rounds. He has 130 customers who depend on him for their milk. And in 21 years, he's never let them down.

Cliff remembers one particularly bad storm on Paris Hill. "About 13 years ago, I had this lady up there," he reminisces. "We happened to have a Nor'easter and I finally got to her place and when I walked in she told me, 'You are the most dependable thing in my life.' That made my day."

As Cliff explains it, his job is much more than just being a milkman. "You pretty much do everything: some-times you put out the dog, bring out the cat. The only thing I don't do is windows and dishes." But he goes further than most: "Three weeks ago a woman down in Oxford Village asked me to put her socks on. That's a good one, huh? And I did it! Unbelievable."

"There's not too many of us left anymore—just getting up in the morning is bad enough," Cliff admits. The hours have rescheduled his whole life. "When I was a kid, in grammar school and high school, I wouldn't go to bed at night, and I wouldn't get up in the morning. When I graduated and went into the service, it turned all around. I went to bed at night, got up in the morning, and I've been getting up ever since."

For 11 years, Cliff has been his own boss, working as an independent distributor for Hood Dairy. "Either I went independent, or I was out on the street," he explains. "That was 11 years ago, and at that time, jobs were pretty scarce up here. And I'd already been doing this for ten years." So Cliff bought the truck, the customer list, and a contract with Hood. He likes the life, but it has its draw-

Milkman Cliff Plourde on his appointed rounds.

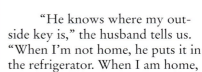

backs—with independence comes no vacation, no retirement plan, and no sick days.

"I had the flu one time, on a Friday, and on Monday I was back to work," he states. "That's what it is about being independent. You can't have everything, but if you like something you have to abide by it and dedicate yourself to it and do it. You got to do it."

The sun is up now. Cliff pulls into the circular drive-way of a handsome Victorian. "Hi Claire!" he hollers. He steps inside a busy kitchen. A phone is ringing, a dog is barking, but Claire is nowhere in sight. Cliff adds "It's me!," as he places Claire's order inside the refrigerator. Then he's off.

Cliff has to work 60 to 80 hours a week to meet his $120,000 yearly expenses. And while the majority of his customers pay on time, some ask for credit. "Things are tough sometimes," he says. "You have to be a little lenient. But being lenient, you usually get caught. That's the way I am—too lenient," he admits. "If I'd be hard, they would probably quit, and I wouldn't have to worry about collecting my money."

At the next house, a husband and wife are having breakfast together. They go on about buttering their toast as Cliff heads for the refrigerator.

"He knows where my outside key is," the husband tells us. "When I'm not home, he puts it in the refrigerator. When I am home, we talk—about fishing, usually." This man knows Cliff well: "He fishes year-round. I've fished with him a couple of times and I can tell you, on the job and off the job, he's still the same character. Always cheerful."

Cliff Plourd belongs to a disappearing breed. It is unlikely that anyone will replace him when he gives up his route. His customers will have to travel 10 to 20 miles to reach the nearest grocery store.

For now, Cliff battles the cold and the unfriendly canines. He may have to put up with their barks, but he also gets his bites—at his final stop of the day, he finds homemade candy left by a satisfied customer.

The solitary life does have its rewards: "You go out in the morning. Nobody's been out there. No tracks on the roads, you're the only one out. Branches are burdened with snow. It's a beautiful sight and a lot of people don't get to see that in a lifetime."

UPDATE: The folks at Hood Dairy tell us that Cliff is retired, living in the Lewiston area, and most likely not getting out of bed until well past sunrise.

HORSE SENSE

Just like stone walls and hardy apple trees, the Morgan horse is
a symbol of New England. Considered America's first horse breed,
the Morgan had inauspicious beginnings: the first of the breed was a runty-looking
colt given to Vermont's Justin Morgan to settle a debt. Yet today, Morgans are
found in all 50 states and in more than 20 foreign countries. In the spring of 1990,
Chronicle visited one of the best-known Morgan farms in New England.

East of Equinox is a picturesque 25-acre Morgan horse farm set in Manchester, in Vermont's southwestern corner. Caring for the farm and its sixty Morgans is a 24-hour-a-day job. But it's clear that manager Ivan Beattie is doing what he loves best.

"I've often said that if I couldn't be associated with Morgan horses, then I wouldn't be associated with horses at all," Ivan declares. "I think Morgans are that much different than other breeds."

Morgans are prized for their intelligence, personality, and, most of all, versatility. "It was a horse you could plow fields with, then hook up to the carriage on a Sunday and take the family to church," Ivan explains. "And you could have friendly wager bets with your friends over who had the fastest horse. If you had the Morgan, you'd probably win."

Among Ivan's 60 horses, he shares a special affinity with his prized 17-year-old stallion, Courage.

"Courage and I are a lot alike; not getting any younger, physically not what we used to be, but still highly regarded in the industry as being very good at what we do," he says.

What Courage does today is breed. In fact, at the time of Chronicle's visit, Courage stood as the world's top-ranked sire of Morgan show horses, commanding a stud fee of $3,000. His foals sold anywhere between $5,000 and $25,000.

"Fifty percent of Courage's offspring have gone on to be great champions in the show ring," Ivan boasts. "This is an unparalleled accomplishment for a stallion."

The farm bustles with activity: horses, family pets, chickens, and the Beatties' three children: ten-year-old Vanessa; eight-year-old Megan; and Matt, age six. Ivan and

The Beattie family on the farm.

his wife Sandy are, above all, realists; they recognize both the sacrifices and rewards of farm life.

"I think growing up on a farm is the best experience a child can have," Ivan says. "Everything from learning a responsibility to just growing up in the outdoors and interacting with horses and other people. I think our kids have a real advantage that way."

Apparently, Vanessa agrees with her dad. "When I grow up," she predicts, "I might get a stallion and a mare and breed them and start a farm for myself." Megan adds, "I'm thinking of just staying here and taking care of the farm."

Ivan grows philosophical as he looks ahead to his children's future and his own legacy. "I wouldn't be doing this if I was in it for the money," he muses. "The hours are long, the pay short, but I think we're really doing something in the Morgan horse breed that will have long-term effects. Generations from now, people will say we made a mark in the Morgan horse breed."

During the Civil War, Morgans served as cavalry mounts and artillery horses.

The First Vermont Cavalry was exclusively mounted on Morgans, and they were considered by many to be the best cavalry mounts in either army. Of those 1,200 Morgans, only 200 survived the war.

UPDATE: Courage continues to break records at the age of 28. He's become the most prolific sire in the history of the Morgan breed, with more registered offspring than any other stallion. And he's extending his own record, at the rate of about 30 mares a year. In addition, Courage is the first stallion to stand at stud simultaneously in the United States, Canada, England, and continental Europe. What's more, he's responsible for the first foal in England to be conceived by frozen semen.

As for the Beattie's three children, now aged 21, 19, and 17, none has plans at this point to join the family business. Ivan has mixed feelings about this. "On one hand, I'd love to see the farm continue to a third generation. On the other hand, I wouldn't wish this work on anybody if they didn't want to do it." Ivan pauses for a moment. "Of course, at their age, I certainly didn't think I'd be doing this—joining my parents on the farm—either!"

PORTRAITS of the PAST

Courtesy: Jo Anne Preston

Twenty-first-century life is the examined life. Children grow up on video-tape. Complete strangers share their bedrooms via Webcams. Modesty seems outmoded. It's a far cry from the 19th century, when portraits had just become something middle-class people could afford. In the summer of 1992, Old Sturbridge Village, a Massachusetts museum, assembled 90 paintings from the era in an exhibit called "Meet Your Neighbors." Each had a story to tell, with themes that are still fresh 150 years later.

They look at us through simple picture frames, and from across time. A single woman, her gaze direct. A family of three, mother with her hair piled high, father in formal wear with a book in his hand, and in between, a baby in a green gown, looking preternaturally old. A bearded black man, formally dressed and proud.

Historian Jessica Nichol finds these images fascinating, and useful. "I think it's the only period in history that we can point to where much more ordinary citizens were commissioning painted portraits, images that were really permanent memorials of who they were," Nichol says. "So for us, they provide a wonderful way of encountering these people in the past—the kind of people that don't tend to be well documented."

Portrait of the Young Artist

Inside an oval frame there is another painting—a self portrait—of a curly haired young man named Nathan Negus.

Nichol says artists like Negus documented pre-Civil War America in their work.

"These itinerant artists are often young men from farm families. They tended to travel through the countryside. Usually, they didn't just go into a town cold. They often would go to a place where they had a family connection or had some friends that could introduce them to people," Nichols explains.

Negus left detailed information about his work in his account books. "Some months were flush, he had hundreds of dollars to send home to help his family out," Nichol reports. "Other months were really lean." In one passage, Negus describes arriving in Fitchburg, Massachusetts, on a Thursday, spending a week doing two portraits, and leaving with his fee: six dollars a painting.

The work could take him anywhere. In 1825, it brought him to Georgia and Alabama. But he was not a well man, having contracted tuberculosis, and he made

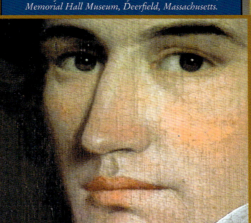

Courtesy: Pocumtuck Valley Memorial Association, Memorial Hall Museum, Deerfield, Massachusetts.

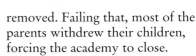

Nathan Negus, above and center. Jessica Nichol, far right.

plans to return to New England. After more than a month stalled at sea, he arrived at his home in Petersham, Massachusetts. He died there three days later. Nathan Negus was 25.

A Pioneer in Education

Another portrait is of a young woman, her eyes intent, her hair pulled back as short as a boy's. This is Prudence Crandall, the daughter of Quakers from Rhode Island, who established a private academy in 1831 on the town common in Canterbury, Connecticut. She taught reading, writing, arithmetic, chemistry, and astronomy, among other subjects, at a tuition of $25 per quarter.

Museum curator Kazimiera Kozlowski says that at first, Crandall received a warm welcome from the town. But then Crandall got a lesson in the morals of her community, courtesy of a young black woman named Sarah Harris. The 20-year-old Harris, interested in training to be a teacher, came looking for admission to the school. In writing about the reaction that news generated, Crandall acknowledged what she was up against. "I saw that the prejudice of whites against color was deep and inveterate."

Townspeople first demanded that Harris be removed. Failing that, most of the parents withdrew their children, forcing the academy to close. After conferring with William Lloyd Garrison and other Abolitionists, Crandall reopened the academy six months later, as a school dedicated exclusively to the education of young black women.

"I said in my heart, here are my convictions. What shall I do?" she wrote. "Shall I be inactive and permit prejudice, the mother of abomination, to remain undisturbed? I contemplated for a while the manner in which I might best serve the people of color. As wealth was not mine, I saw no other means of benefiting them. . . . This I deem my duty."

Students came from across New England to attend the new academy. Local reaction was swift, as Kozlowski describes. "Many of the shopkeepers won't sell to the school. At one point, there was manure put down the well. Now, she couldn't get clean drinking water, and you needed that on a day to day basis. There were dead cats placed on the fence out front, the house was splattered with mud and eggs. The town realized they had to do something a little broader to stop what was going on and began distributing petitions, basically saying that they

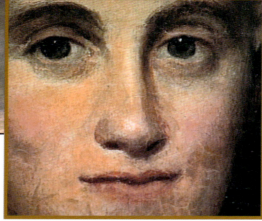

Prudence Crandall, above and right.

want a law passed to close the school down."

Five weeks after the re-opening of the school, the Connecticut Legislature obliged opponents by passing a law that made it illegal to educate "any colored people . . . not inhabitants" of Connecticut. Within days of the enactment of the so-called Black Law, Prudence Crandall was arrested.

Crandall spent a night in jail, and endured three trials. In the last one, the judge threw the case out of court, saying the Black Law could not deprive citizens of their rights to an education. The legal fight over, the school was back in operation—until the night of Sept 9, 1834. Kozlowski describes what happened.

"A mob attacked the school that evening. A local group of men with bars and clubs and stones did as much damage as they could to the exterior of the building. Luckily, no one within the school was injured. But Prudence decided to close the school."

Although Crandall fled Connecticut under attack, she did live to see vindication when the Black Law was repealed in 1838. In 1886, at the urging of supporters, including Mark Twain, the Connecticut Legislature granted her a pension. Ripples from her resistance were felt well into the 20th century; arguments from her trials were used in the U.S. Supreme Court's school desegregation decision of 1954.

In 1890, at the age of 87, Prudence Crandall died. But curator Kozlowski insists that the lesson of her life remains timely.

"If we have that strength, that inner strength, to go with what we personally feel is right, what is morally correct, then we can accomplish things that we probably would never think that we would be capable of doing."

Steadfast Sisters

One final portrait at the Sturbridge exhibit is of two women, sisters born into a farming family, each with their hand on what looks like a Bible. They are Hannah and Mary Adams, distant relatives to Jo Anne Preston, a writer who tells their story with visible pride.

"Contrary to the popular belief that women were to be domestic and stay at home, these women developed their own lives," Preston declares. "You can tell by the way they write their letters that they are very excited and they feel fulfilled, and that they are pioneers."

Mary Adams got an apprenticeship with a tailor in

Jo Anne Preston

Kazimiera Kozlowski

Nashua, New Hampshire, as a way to achieve her real goal—starting a business of her own. In an 1832 letter to Mr. Hickey, the tailor, she made certain both parties understood the arrangement.

"But to prevent future discord and unpleasant feeling therefore," she wrote, "I wish to understand whether you will learn me the whole of the tailoring trade in such a manner that I might, at the expiration of 18 months, be able to cut, make up, and press off any cloth entrusted to my care in a workmanlike manner. And, if possible, to the satisfaction of customers."

Preston picks up the story.

"As months go by, Mister Hickey hasn't taught her the one critical skill that she needs, which is to cut out the patterns. And her family begins to write to her with great concern that, as they wrote, she would be nothing but a shop girl her entire life. So she might as well come home now, because she would never be able to have her own business. But Mary perseveres and finally, after 19 months in an 18-month apprenticeship, she learns how to cut."

Armed with her new knowledge, Mary teamed up with Hannah to open a tailoring shop in Manchester, New Hampshire. In an 1841 letter, Hannah wrote home with good news: business was booming.

Dear Father and Mother,

As it respects ourselves, we are as happy as pigs in the clover. Nothing to do but work. And of that, we are overrun. After we lay our work aside, we have plenty of intellectual enjoyment. Books and papers, meetings and lectures. I think we are the most happily situated of any persons in our knowledge.

Your dutiful daughter,
Hannah Adams

Jo Anne Preston sees the story of these two women as the story of a generation beginning to sample the fruits of freedom.

"Hannah and Mary and other women who were similarly situated viewed these new employment opportunities as an option to marriage. Not that they were dead set against it, but unlike their mothers, they were not required to get married to have an adult life."

Neither sister married. They ran their business for more than 50 years, bought stock, and owned real estate. The portrait they commissioned shows two self-assured, independent women. And the book they're holding that looks like a Bible? It's actually one of their account books, tangible proof of all that they had accomplished.

PLACES

WINNIPESAUKEE WINTER

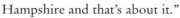

Wolfeboro, New Hampshire, bills itself as America's oldest summer resort, and the crowds that walk along the shore of Lake Winnipesaukee in June, July, and August are testament to its continuing popularity. But Peter Mehegan found a different atmosphere when he visited in the winter of 1991.

Think of the magical, "lost" communities of legend and lore. Brigadoon, the Scottish village that appears once a century—or Shangri-la. Now consider New Hampshire's corollary to these mythical places: Fisherville.

But Fisherville is not a myth. It's a town, first built in the 1920s, and recognized by the state in 1937. You'll find it on Lake Winnipesaukee, but only in winter, and only after the lake freezes.

Carl Shannon, Fisherville's assistant mayor, is glad to give the grand tour: the town hall, the post office, and a school that specializes in one subject—how to make a fire. Carl also shows off a new addition: a chapel, complete with pew, inspirational literature, and a floor that's . . . holey.

It doesn't take long to divine that those gathered here are used to unanswered prayers. They are ice fishermen. Some enter the annual ice fishing derby, with more than $40,000 at stake. Others are content to sit and tell stories, sit and play cards, sit and eat, sit and—oh yeah—fish.

"Some of the wives don't know we're here," admits one visitor from Maine. "They know we're in New Hampshire and that's about it."

Is it safe to set up housekeeping on the ice? That depends on the state of your marriage. But as far as fretting about landing at the bottom of the lake, Carl says not to worry—the ice is 13 inches thick. Driving can get interesting, though, as Carl discovered one time when he took his brand new truck out on a dock. "Down I went, right to the bottom, truck and all," Carl says. "Truck was only four months old. Now we call it my submarine, because it has gone down and it has come up."

Llama Love

If solid ground sounds inviting after that story, you can head inland to Llongneck Llama Farm. Owner Caroline Boeckman-Dunne used to live in Boston and worked at the Franklin Park Zoo. But after her car was broken into three times, she decided she needed to make a change. "I wasn't sure what to do with my life but I knew I wasn't really happy with what I was doing," she says. Her father mentioned an airline magazine article about llamas. She

Carl Shannon, left, the gang arriving by the vanload, and a l'il 'fry, just chillin' in Dad's icehouse, far right.

did her reading, then breeding, and today presides over the largest llama farm in New Hampshire.

It sounds like a pretty good gig. Caroline says llamas are gentle, don't eat a lot, and are easier to care for than dogs. Caroline breeds llamas for sale as pack or work animals, and also sells the wool. She also takes them to local nursing homes where they bond quickly with residents. But that's not all. Her most unique product is made from a farm by-product that's been dried and varnished and turned into llama poop necklaces. One consumer note: they are not recommended as an accessory on a hot day.

Party of One

Finally, the itinerary moves from llama to Cow . . . Island. That's where you find George Randall, a self-proclaimed hermit. He lives all alone on the island during the winter,

doing maintenance on the summer cottages there. He's got his books, his wood stove, and his truck—complete with the license plate ARGH.

Living in the middle of Winnipesaukee in winter takes planning. "When you've forgotten mayonnaise—in the case of wimpy ice in the spring or the fall or whatever —you're going to do without it for four weeks, or five weeks, or even six weeks," George explains.

But for all the hardships and extra precautions, he can't imagine living anywhere else.

UPDATE: After 13 years of expanding her llama ranch business, Caroline Boeckman-Dunne decided to sell the ranch and relocate to Massachusetts. The move was for family reasons, not because she was sick of llamas. In fact, she took eight of them with her to her new home.

WOODBURY: WHERE NEW ENGLAND BEGINS

Though it's just 90 minutes north of New York City, Woodbury is as New England as Vermont or New Hampshire. In fact, some say this western Connecticut town is where New England truly begins. With more than forty antique shops, Woodbury has earned the title of Connecticut's antiques capital. And, the town has another distinction, as Chronicle found out when we visited in 1992: movie icon Marilyn Monroe once made her home here.

Malteds, Marilyn, and More

From penny candy to prescriptions to pinwheels, you can find just about anything at Canfield's Corner Pharmacy, Connecticut's oldest drugstore. Canfield's still does business the old-fashioned way. Local children make their selections from overstocked shelves, then run a tab on their candy and sodas. The daily paper is set aside for playwright Arthur Miller and other local residents. And this is one drugstore where home delivery is not a thing of the past.

Leaning across a well-worn linoleum counter, owner and druggist Vera Elsenboss describes the Canfield business philosophy. "We offer merchandise and psychological support," she says. "We are the old-fashioned, traditional, caring pharmacy."

Vera recalls a number of famous Canfield customers. She claims that during Marilyn Monroe's marriage to

Arthur Miller, Marilyn's favorite spot was the corner stool at the old soda fountain. "I didn't recognize her the first time she came in; Arthur introduced her," Vera recalls. "She didn't look like Marilyn Monroe. Marilyn on the screen is a big girl, but Marilyn in person was very small. And very kind. And she always bought the cheapest she could find—I guess she remembered the times when she didn't have a penny."

Main Street Makeover

Time has been good to Woodbury. On Main Street, you won't find a McDonald's, a mall, or even a movie theater. What you will find are lots and lots of antiques. But furniture and china aren't the only attraction. At least as interesting are the dealers themselves. Take Madeleine West—the owner of Madeleine West Antiques. When *The New York Times* once called her "slightly eccentric," she was quick to

Woodbury's various treasures, including Wayne Mattox and his table.

voice her objection. "I told them I was *totally* eccentric—I'm never *slightly* anything!"

When Madeleine first set up shop 35 years ago, houses along Main Street were not as well cared for as they are today. But Main Street neatened up *and* became a bona fide neighborhood because of a change in zoning laws that requires shopkeepers to live where they work. According to Nancy Heubner, president of the Antiques Dealers Association and owner of Carriage House Antiques, the change is a bonus for visitors. "They get double the entertainment value. They get to look at the beautiful antiques, and the beautiful homes as well."

Heubner's home, built circa 1720, is a perfect backdrop for her merchandise. "We found that we didn't really utilize the second floor of the house except to play piano, so we thought it would be a perfect setting for the antiques," she explains. "It serves as a wonderful backdrop to put pieces of this period in a home where you would have seen them originally."

Another well-known dealer is Wayne Mattox, co-owner of his family's shop, Daria of Woodbury. "One of the things I like most about this business are the people we deal with every day. They're wackos."

Wayne insists his remark is a compliment to the tastes of his customers. "The people who buy antiques from us don't want to be exactly like their neighbors next door. They want to express their personality."

It took a long time for Wayne to develop his own taste for antiques. It was years before he joined the family business. "I grew up thinking this stuff was dusty and inelegant. I never really appreciated it," he admits.

Now he knows a good thing when he sees it—like the table he spied in a dusty field at the Brimfield flea market. "It was made in the Philadelphia area around 1815. There's perhaps 20 of them known to exist," Wayne discloses. "The dealer who had it knew what it was, and charged me a fortune—$11,000. I was a nervous wreck after I bought it."

Wayne phoned home after he struck the deal. His mother, Daria Mattox, still remembers the call. "Eleven thousand dollars for a table up at Brimfield!?! I couldn't believe it! But I thought to myself, 'Well, look, the house is paid for, the kids have turned out fine . . . there's worse things that can happen than losing eleven thousand dollars.'"

But Daria's thinking changed when she laid eyes on the prize. "He brought the table inside and it was magnificent," she recalls. "It was worth a lot more than he paid."

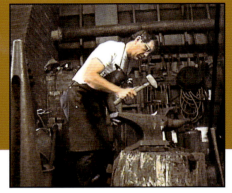

Woodbury's blacksmith Charlie Euston, Woodbury Pewter, and the Calder property.

Ye Olde Craftsmen

If Woodbury's antique shops don't yield that old widget you need, you might want to call on Charlie Euston. He's the town's blacksmith, and his shop is right on Main Street.

"We are a shop very much like the 18th-century shop," Charlie says. "We still get people from town who come just to watch. Some bring their broken kettles or other implements to be repaired."

Charlie was a teacher who took up blacksmithing as a hobby. When he got involved in restoring an old blacksmith shop, he was hooked. "One day I went over the edge and took it up full-time," he says. "I was told that you won't make a million being a blacksmith—and that much is obvious now. But I can totally say I love what I do."

When Charlie's phone rings, it might be an order for a single door handle, or for hardware to outfit an entire house. He also gets calls from purists who want four or five thousand nails to build a house.

Also on Main Street, another old craft enjoys a revival at Woodbury Pewter. Second-generation pewterer Brooks Titcomb takes pride in his family's business, founded in 1952. "I think a lot of the appeal is that it's handmade. We do all the processes right in the shop."

The company started out with just a handful of designs, styled after wares by the most famous of pewterers: Revere, Danforth, and Boardman. Today, more than 450 different items stock the shelves. The hottest seller is customized pewter. "A number of the large corporations in the area take a great deal of pride in taking a piece of Woodbury pewter abroad," he says. "They like to say 'This is where we come from.' So 'Made in Woodbury' shows up in Japan, Germany, Australia—all over."

But this corner of Connecticut isn't completely steeped in early American history. Travel the back roads and you'll find a surprise. In the hill town of Roxbury is the home of the late sculptor Alexander Calder. From the road you can see the whimsical moving sculptures which still decorate the property.

Summer Sleigh Ride

The ever-popular melody "Sleigh Ride" is as much a part of wintertime as snowmen and Santa Claus. But few who know the piece also know that it was written by the late composer, Leroy Anderson, during a Woodbury summertime heat wave (not exactly lovely weather for a sleigh ride together!). Anderson first discovered the peaceful, wooded Litchfield Hills in the late 1940s. Soon after, he and his

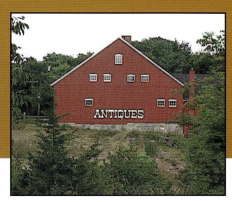

Composer Leroy Anderson and his bandstand.

wife, Eleanor, decided to make the area their permanent home. Anderson died here in 1975, but Mrs. Anderson still lives in the home they built on a tranquil hillside. "Everyone can hum his tunes, and yet they're not always sure who composed them," Mrs. Anderson says. "I think that happens to music that's very popular. You could say his music is part of the fabric of American life."

It's this popularity that inspired Mrs. Anderson to contact the United States Postmaster and propose that her late husband be honored with a stamp, joining the ranks of Dizzy Dean and Elvis Presley. "The craftsmanship of his music was so high, and it was highly thought of," she says. "People also admired his ability to orchestrate, and the originality of his melodies."

Music lovers from all over the country have written letters of support for the stamp. They say that Anderson's is the kind of music that simply makes you smile. "Just listen to 'Sleigh Ride' or 'Syncopated Clock,'" she says. "Doesn't that make you happy?"

Mrs. Anderson believes her husband would be proud to have his face on a postage stamp. "He knew his music would last."

Anderson's neighbors knew it too. Down on Main Street, the Leroy Anderson bandstand stands ready and waiting for the next concert on the green—just another piece of life in Woodbury.

UPDATE: Eleanor Anderson's dream has not yet been realized. She reports that nearly a decade later, her request is still under consideration by the Postal Service in Washington, D.C.

We have better news from Wayne Mattox, who reports that he sold his table for "something in the range of $25,000." Though he won't reveal the name of the buyer, he does add that over the years, his shop has been visited by a number of "celebrity browsers," including Whoopi Goldberg, Jane Fonda, and Harrison Ford.

For further information and listings of Woodbury antique dealers, check the Woodbury Antiques Dealers Association Web site, www.antiqueswoodbury.com, or write to Woodbury Antiques Dealers Association, P.O. Box 496, Woodbury, CT 06798.

The MOUNT WASHINGTON HOTEL

The Mount Washington Hotel is one of the last examples of New England's grand hotels. While others have succumbed to financial troubles, fires, and neglect, The Mount Washington is still standing. But there have been times when its survival was in doubt. In 1992, Chronicle documented the hotel's near death and rebirth. And in 2000, we witnessed a new chapter in its long history.

June 26, 1991. A jewel of the Granite State is on the auction block. The Mount Washington Hotel, a fixture of the White Mountain National Forest landscape for a century, is put up for sale by the Federal Deposit Insurance Corporation, owners by default after foreclosure. The expected high bid: eight million dollars.

It's a far cry from the glory days of this grand dame. The saga started in 1900, when New Hampshire native Joseph Stickney, a rail and coal tycoon, broke ground to build his grand obsession. Stickney had earlier gone to Italy and hand picked 250 artisans, housing them on the grounds as they built the structure over the course of two years. When it opened, it joined a group of about 30 grand hotels within 25 miles of Mount Washington. As many as 50 trains a day carried wealthy guests from Boston, New York, and Philadelphia into the three stations at nearby Bretton Woods. Many arrived to spend the whole summer season in the luxury of the hotel.

The roster of guests included Thomas Edison, Babe Ruth, Joseph P. Kennedy, Alfred Hitchcock, Winston Churchill, and John D. Rockefeller, who reportedly awarded his caddy with a tip of one dime. Vanderbilts strolled the famous veranda. And financial history was made here. In June of 1944, a world monetary conference at the hotel established the gold standard and instituted the International Monetary Fund and the World Bank.

The White Elephant In the White Mountains

But the golden age did not last. Experts say the automobile killed the era of the grand hotels in the White Mountains. It became too easy for "commoners" to get there; the wealthy vacationers who wanted luxury and exclusivity in equal measure began to go elsewhere. One by one The Mount Washington's neighbors closed.

The hotel was placed on the National Register of Historic Places in 1978 and achieved a National Historic Landmark designation in 1986. Although it remained a popular destination, it needed extensive restoration. Some

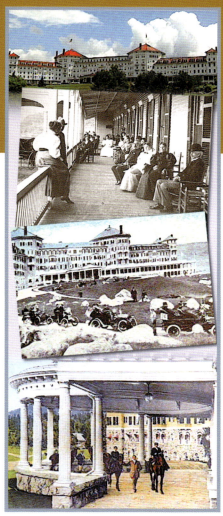

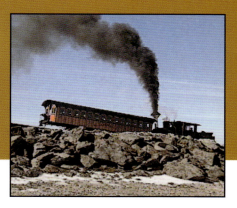

The hotel then and now, complete with cog railway.

wags began calling it the "White Elephant in the White Mountains." After passing through the hands of multiple owners in the 1980s, The Mount Washington was acquired in 1990 by the FDIC, which spent a million dollars on refurbishments. Then came the June 1991 auction. A team of New Hampshire partners took the prize at the bargain price of just over $3 million. A new chapter in the hotel's history had begun.

Today, The Mount Washington Resort includes a country inn, a motor inn, cog railway, ski area, and golf courses, as well as the grand hotel, all surrounded by 18,000 acres of the White Mountain National Forest. In 1999, the hotel's owners took a step into the new century with a radical idea: opening for winter. All it took was replacing 900 windows, buying 8,000 gallons of oil to heat the 200 guest rooms, and convincing guests that a summer resort could indeed learn new tricks.

Courtesy: The Mount Washington Hotel

Talking Heads?

Is The Mount Washington Hotel haunted? Some old timers report sightings of a woman who walks through walls and disappears. In the strangest incident, unexplained slashes appeared one day on many of the photographs hanging in the hotel. One theory: it's the ghost of the wife of hotel founder Joseph Stickney.

In the winter of 1999, the hotel's hospitality manager and his wife spent each night in a different room to personally test the new heating system throughout the building. They didn't see or hear anything out of the ordinary until early one morning when they were awakened by a knocking from inside a closet. They opened the door to find a man's head on the floor smiling up at them. It was a workman who had broken through the ceiling from below while working on the pipes.

LIFE *on* SEBAGO LAKE

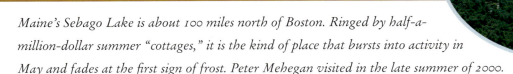

Maine's Sebago Lake is about 100 miles north of Boston. Ringed by half-a-million-dollar summer "cottages," it is the kind of place that bursts into activity in May and fades at the first sign of frost. Peter Mehegan visited in the late summer of 2000.

At 46 square miles, Sebago Lake is not Maine's largest lake; that honor goes to Moosehead. But it is the state's most popular, and in summer, the most populated. Since it's mostly private property along the water, you have to be creative to get the whole picture.

Peter managed to find a great way to see Sebago: from the air, aboard Jacki Rogers's seaplane.

"In the state of Maine, there is so much water that if you get to an altitude of about three thousand feet, you've got a runway anywhere in the state," Jacki explains.

"It's a lot of fun, the challenge of taking off and landing on water and doing the sailing of an aircraft on the water. It's the landing that can be a little on the tricky side. You can't judge distance quite as much, so you have to come in at a slower rate of descent. That's my favorite—landing—actually."

If you prefer to stay closer to the shore, the deck of the *Songo River Queen,* a paddle wheeler cruising out of the town of Naples, may feel like a safer choice. Its path down the Songo River twists and turns, appropriate on a river also known as the "Little Snake."

The journey takes passengers past the last hand-operated bridge in Maine, and then into the Songo River Lock, also hand operated since it was built in 1830. At that time, it was part of the Cumberland and Oxford Canal, connecting Sebago Lake with Portland.

Captain Casey Chase and his wife, Sally, began operating the boat in 1985. But listen up, you folks with maritime in your marrow. According to Sally, they're ready to give up the ship.

"Well, she's for sale. Three hundred seventy-five thousand gets you the boat, the business, and a lot of fun."

Landscaping—Sebago-style

Local historian Ernie Knight knows some of the more interesting sites around Sebago. There's the boyhood home of author Nathaniel Hawthorne, and the cave he played in as a child. There's also the cliff known for its Native American paintings. But we thought his best yarn was the one about a farmer named David McClellan.

The story goes that McClellan didn't like the shadow thrown on his home by nearby Rattlesnake Mountain. So he hired local handyman Edgar Welch to take the peak down a few pegs. Welch's solution: he went

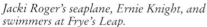

Jacki Roger's seaplane, Ernie Knight, and swimmers at Frye's Leap.

straight to the top.

"So he undertook to cut down the height of the mountain by rolling the rocks over," Ernie reveals. "People used to wake up in the middle of the night and hear the boulders rolling."

Ernie also points out the cliff known as Frye's Leap, named after a soldier who jumped off the precipice to escape an American Indian attack. Captain Joseph Frye then swam to the largest island on the lake, which now also bears his name. In 1998, Frye Island officially became Maine's newest town.

Ebb and Flow

The water level of the lake is a constant concern for the residents of Sebago. Boaters want it high for the best clearance; landowners want it low so the shoreline won't erode. You can see who's winning at Sebago Lake State Park, where a once popular beach is now underwater. Park Ranger Dick Jordan has watched the beach disappear slowly over the years.

"Back in the '50s this beach would be back out here another 250 feet or so," he says, pointing toward the lake.

"To the best of my recollection, this started about 1986." "I think it's a shame the way it looks. Maybe someday we'll be bringing it back to the way it was."

He prefers to stress the positive, though.

"We've got 62 miles of running water for boaters here, fishing is starting to pick back up. It's just a paradise."

Peter decides to check out the fishing himself. Shortly after dawn, he joins Captain Yvon Duquette. At this time of year, with an autumn chill already setting in, there is little competition from other anglers. Captain Yvon likes it that way.

"What a nice morning," he exclaims. "Look at that sun. I like nature. It feels good to be with nature. If we're lucky, we catch a fish. This time of year you have to work."

The quarry is a lake trout called togue. The weapons include traditional bait, and electronics.

"You go deep with fish finders. It's not right but everybody does it," Yvon admits.

He does find some trout on the fish finder, a device

that works like sonar to search the depths. But none will take their bait. So, instead of continuing with the futility of fishing present, Peter looks up Bill Weeks for some stories of fishing past.

Camp Conversions

Bill's family once owned the Thompson Fishing Camps. In the 1930s, fishermen came to places like the camps in search of salmon.

"If you caught a fish, it was 99 percent sure to be a salmon, and to catch much else in there was quite unusual," Weeks says. "The amazing thing is that these men would row all day. They would row that boat four, five, six miles just to get to where they wanted to fish, row all day trolling, and row back in the afternoon."

Weeks says that as time went on, the crowd changed. "Those fishermen thought it was a great place and thought they ought to bring their wives. So, as years went on the wives came and then their children," he explains. "So when it got to the 50s, it evolved from a pure fishing proposition to more of a classy resort."

In 1960, the Thompson family sold the property, which was then carved up and redeveloped as summer homes. It can take a pretty penny to get into those "cottages" today, with some in the half-million-dollar-and-up category. Joyce Barter of Krainin Real Estate knows the lay of the land.

"There are only 15 places on the lake right now, from $180,000 to $900,000," she says. "You can't develop the beach any more and that's what makes these places so desirable."

That price also gets you up close and personal with one of the most strictly controlled water districts in New England. The southern end of Sebago provides the water for Portland and nine other nearby communities. Within a two-mile radius of the intake pipe, no bodily contact with the water is allowed. In other words, it's safe to drink the water—just don't dip your toes.

U P D A T E : Songo River Queen celebrated its 20th season in 2001. Sally Chase says it's still for sale.

The BERKSHIRES' GILDED AGE

Courtesy: Lenox Library

In summer, Lenox and Stockbridge, Massachusetts, are abuzz with visitors who flock to Tanglewood, America's premiere music festival, and to other cultural attractions such as the Norman Rockwell Museum. But long before music dominated the Berkshire landscape, the westernmost outpost of Massachusetts was a summer retreat for American industrialists. One by one they built their vacation cottages, and the Berkshires became a showcase for grand displays of wealth—the jewels of American aristocracy. Chronicle chose the spring of 1989, a less-traveled time, to take its tour of the Berkshire Cottages.

The so-called cottages of the Berkshires were, in fact, magnificent mansions. Today, they've been converted into schools, religious retreats, health spas, condominiums, and inns. But once they were summer homes for the wealthy and famous from New York and Boston, financial barons that included names like Carnegie, Vanderbilt, and Westinghouse.

These "cottagers" named their anything-but-modest retreats "Belle Fontaine," "Wheatleigh," "Elm Court," and "Blantyre." So grand were these houses that the Berkshires became known as the inland Newport. The history of the time is preserved in the historical room at the Stockbridge Library. "A lot of people spent the summers in Newport and then they came out here for the fall which, of course, was the best season," explains curator Polly Pierce. Pierce says there was a big difference between the cottages of Stockbridge and Lenox. "Joseph Hodges Choate was a prominent attorney and former ambassador to England, and when he was asked why he picked Stockbridge

instead of Lenox, he said, 'In Lenox you are estimated; in Stockbridge you are esteemed.'"

A Sculptor's Six Months in Heaven

Sadly, what remains today of those formal ballrooms, formidable homes, and fantastic gardens is but a fraction of what once graced this rural landscape. Those cottages that have survived, like Chesterwood, the summer home of sculptor Daniel Chester French, have stories to tell.

French is best known for his "Seated Lincoln," the centerpiece of the Lincoln Memorial that graces the mall in our nation's capital. On display in his Stockbridge studio are the three clay models that trace the evolution of that famous sculpture.

To understand how French was convinced to take up summer residence in Stockbridge, you need only look at the majestic views of Monument Mountain. According to Paul Ivory, Chesterwood's director, French called his time there his "six months in heaven." "We're unique because

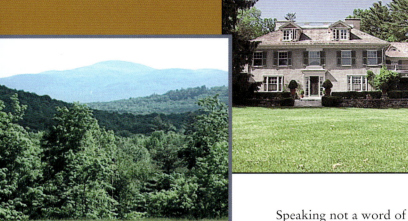

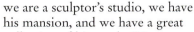

Chesterwood, home of sculptor Daniel Chester French.

we are a sculptor's studio, we have his mansion, and we have a great collection of his works," Ivory says. "It gives a rich insight into the everyday existence of America's foremost sculptor of public monuments."

Chesterwood has been preserved as an historic landmark, but not every old estate can be elevated to such status.

"You can't make every old mansion a museum, it isn't economically feasible, it isn't practical," Ivory acknowledges. "That's where the big challenge comes in, trying to find uses for them so that they are preserved but also can contribute to the economy."

Cottage Industry

Extravagant as they may seem today, the cottages not only completed a lifestyle, they were good for the local economy. Huge staffs were employed to care for the grounds and the houses, sometimes as many as fifty people for a household of two.

In 1923, Francine Darey and her family moved from Brittany in France to Lenox. "Everything was so beautiful, all the estates and the town was kept just beautifully too," she recalls.

Speaking not a word of English and desperately homesick, Mrs. Darey sought employment as a maid at a cottage named Stonover. "It was important to them, you see, how they dressed, how their bedroom looked, what they were going to eat for lunch, where they were going to play tennis, those kind of things."

The End of an Era

But it wasn't long before the bottom dropped out of this privileged existence. Suddenly, on one dark Tuesday in 1929, the rich weren't so rich anymore. First Darey lost her job; then she suffered a greater tragedy. Her husband of two years died, leaving her with a nine-month-old baby. Salvation appeared in the form of a local shopkeeper who offered her a job, in a store she would one day own. Among her customers were the cottagers.

"When they had money they were at the store all the time and when they had no money they came to the store just the same," she says. "I remember one woman saying, 'I can't afford a cook and I can't even boil water. I can't cook an egg!' and she put her head down and she was crying."

In these desperate times many cottages were forced

Blantyre, Lenox Selectman George Darey, and a theater group at The Mount.

out of private ownership. One exception is a property now known as Highlawn Farm, home to Marjorie Field Wilde. If you're traveling north from Stockbridge to Lenox, you can see the farm from Route 7. Hidden beyond the barns and pastures is the gracious Highlawn House. The farm was all once part of a 900-acre estate that included Elm Court, built by Mrs. Wilde's grandmother, Emily Thorn Vanderbilt Sloane.

The farm has been in operation since before 1900. Mrs. Wilde is a master breeder of Jerseys. Beaming with pride, she introduces one of her favorites, a cow named Ginger whose lineage traces back 11 generations to the original Highlawn herd.

"I like her the best," she exclaims. "She's just a very nice old cow, very high protein, which is the thing that everybody wants in the way of milk."

Resurrecting with Style

Just down the road in Lenox is Blantyre, an Elizabethan cottage that for years was nothing more than a white elephant. Now, its turn-of-the-century elegance is back, thanks to Jane Fitzpatrick, owner of Stockbridge's famous Red Lion Inn.

"Everything needed fixing. It was sort of a fantasy for me, who was born on a farm in Vermont," Fitzpatrick says. "It allowed me to play out my fantasies and buy sort of extravagant furniture. I love it! For example, we have a cupboard that was in Arthur Fiedler's living room in Brookline."

Today's Blantyre is a high-priced luxury inn. Jane Fitzpatrick believes the cottages are a historic legacy to be treasured, and she is saddened by those that have been abandoned and left to decay.

"I'd rather have it turned into a good condominium than not have it turned into anything," she declares. "A few have been bought for private families. It's a lucky house that gets bought for that reason. This, I think, is the next best reason, running an inn because you can make so many people happy."

House of Worth

Author Edith Wharton spent summers at another Lenox "cottage," The Mount, where she wrote her celebrated novels *Ethan Frome* and *The House of Mirth.* After many years as a private school for girls, there was a proposal to convert The Mount to condominiums. Lenox Selectman George Darey, who had once worked as a caretaker at the home, joined the fight to preserve it.

"Keep Lenox Green, a group of people that wanted to preserve the town of Lenox, finally said, 'Hey, you're

The Mount, the Stockbridge Bowl, and Spring Lawn.

not going to build condominiums here, we're going to stop this,'" Darey recalls.

The opponents won. That meant that the theater group Shakespeare & Company could continue to use the site for its productions of Shakespeare and its re-creations of the world of Edith Wharton.

Magnetic Mansion

The battle to save another Berkshire treasure was not so straightforward. For years the Lenox School for Boys sat on a 63-acre campus that had once been part of the cottages era.

By the mid-1980s, the compound had been taken over by a religious group, Bible Speaks, as its headquarters. One of the group's members was Betsy Doveydenas, a Minneapolis department store heiress who had moved to Lenox with her husband, Jonas. He recalls why the couple chose the Berkshires as their new home. "There's a magnetism here, that's as good an explanation as any, some kind of magnet," he says. "All the things that are necessary for a satisfying life are here."

But in 1987, happiness in their new home was marred when their involvement with Bible Speaks resulted in a highly publicized trial. The Doveydenases, claiming Betsy had been led astray by a greedy pastor,

sued the leader, Carl Stevens, to reclaim $6.5 million she had given to the church. The outcome was a ruling that forced the sale of the property at auction. In a strange twist, the highest bidder, at $1.8 million, was Jonas Doveydenas.

"We wanted to see the property developed in a way that we would be proud of," he explains. "And as residents of Lenox we saw that some of the things that the people who were interested in the property had in mind weren't what we would have wanted in this town."

Doveydenas wants to see a year-round performing arts center and hopes to find just the right buyer for two cottages on the property.

"They were built in the prime of Lenox life and they are wonderful examples of American architecture," he stresses. "I hope we will find a buyer who will use them for what they are—wonderful historic relics.

Mr. Tanglewood

One of the Berkshires' best known names also has a connection to the cottages. The word "Tanglewood" was the creation of author Nathaniel Hawthorne. He used it as the title of a collection of stories he wrote while renting a small house on the Tappan family estate overlooking the Stockbridge Bowl. The name stuck and was later adopted

Jim Kiley, aka "Mr. Tanglewood"

by the owners. In 1936, the property was donated to the Boston Symphony Orchestra and the name Tanglewood became synonymous with music on a summer night.

Longtime caretaker Jim Kiley—"Mr. Tanglewood" to many—spends the long Berkshire winters readying the expansive property for the thousands of visitors that descend each summer. Kiley is the man who not only keeps the carpet-like grass green but carefully guards the legacy at the root of the Tanglewood tradition.

"I believe maintenance is the best insurance you can have on these old buildings and we try to keep them looking as they looked in the past," he states. "It is a big job and the older they get, the harder it is to maintain them."

UPDATE: Jonas Doveydenas did realize, for a short time, his dream of a performing arts center at the old Lenox School for Boys campus. Then, an ambitious attempt to establish a National Music Center on the same site failed. Currently, the property is the new home of Shakespeare & Company. One of the two cottages on the compound is being used for performances; the other is now the privately owned Kemble Inn.

The ownership of Highlawn Farm passed on to the six children of Mrs. Wilde after her death. Together they are working on upgrading the property, which continues

Another Lenox cottage under restoration is Ventfort Hall, an 1893 mansion that sat vacant for many years, nearly suffering irreparable damage. In 1994, a group of local citizens took up the cause, buying the property and raising funds to restore it with the ultimate goal of turning it into the "Museum of the Gilded Age at Ventfort Hall." In 1999, the building played a major role in the Oscar-winning film, The Cider House Rules. *The exterior and main hallway were used as the setting for the orphanage. Ventfort Hall is an official project of Save America's Treasures and is listed on the National Register of Historic Places.*

to be a working dairy farm. The nearly century-old operation now has a brand new milking parlor, something Mrs. Wilde always wanted. Elm Court also remains in the family and is currently being restored after having been vacant for 45 years. The 96-room cottage is one of the most important examples of a shingle-style house in America.

"Mr. Tanglewood," Jim Kiley, died in February 1991.

WANDERING THROUGH WISCASSET

Most travelers using Route 1 in Maine pass straight through Wiscasset on their way to summer vacation destinations, without stopping for a visit. In 1995, Peter Mehegan decided to see what they were missing. What he discovered was a pair of aging schooners, a musical museum, and Red's Eats, where the lobster rolls weigh in at over a pound—all in a town that has good reason to call itself "the prettiest village in Maine."

According to immodest signs at the border, there's no prettier village in Maine than this one. The claim is tough to dispute, once you've glimpsed the stately old sea captains' homes, the picture-perfect town green, and the splintered remains of two four-mastered schooners sitting on the tidal flats of the Sheepscot River.

The ghostly schooners are Wiscasset's calling card. "Eastman Kodak should have paid years ago to have those restored," exclaims selectman Larry Gordon, "because we have more pictures taken of those boats than anything I've ever seen."

Dubbed "Hesper" and "Little Luther," the schooners have been sitting on the riverbank since 1932, when they were dumped by a railroad baron gone bust. In the late 1970s, a group of citizens tried to raise funds to restore the rotting ships. But apparently, natives are not as enamored as visitors; the effort failed. "I believe in death with dignity," long-time resident Marguerite Rafter explains, "and those two should have been dead long ago."

Enticing Eats

Travelers may also know Wiscasset for Red's Eats, a tiny crimson shack at the bottom of Main Street with what *Downeast* magazine calls "the best lobster roll in Maine." Owner Al "they-all-call-me-Red" Gagnon is on the job 18 hours a day—flipping, frying, and serving up french fries to the 500 daily customers who visit his window. As for those famed lobster rolls, Al loads each with a full pound of meat and charges a very fair $10.

Less appetizing but more profitable is one of Wiscasset's leading occupations: worm digging. With long-pronged rakes, diggers turn the Sheepscot River mudflats at low tide, hoping for a bucketful. Wiscasset sea worms

Wiscasset's finest at Red's Eats, "worming" the mudflats, and the Musical Wonder House.

are used by fishermen all over the country.

This is back-breaking work, but it pays off. "I pay 'em by the worm," explains one wholesaler. "These are 13 cents apiece, and I pay 'em on the spot." Worm diggers are tight-lipped on the subject, but word is they can make between $200 and $400 a day.

Magical Musical Tour

Up on Wiscasset's High Street sits a doorway to another era, the Musical Wonder House. This 1852 sea captain's house is now home to thousands of 19th-century mechanical music boxes. Danilo Konvalinka is obviously—and justifiably—proud of his collection. "In the *Michelin International Tour Guide*, we have only one star less than Disney World and the Eiffel Tower!" he boasts. "Still, I think we should have as many as the Eiffel Tower!"

Konvalinka has dedicated 40 years to acquiring and restoring his music boxes. He started collecting in 1957, the year he moved to the United States from his native Austria.

Legend has it that early in the 19th century, Moses Carleton, a Wiscasset shipping magnate, threw his gold ring into the Sheepscot River and boasted, "There's as much chance of my dying a poor man as there is of ever finding that ring again."

Two weeks later, Carleton found his ring inside a fish served at his table. And when President William Henry Harrison embargoed American ships after the British imprisoned American seamen, Carleton died a poor man.

He's lost count of how many music boxes he owns, but he's certain the thousands he has are not enough. "Once you have too many pieces to fit into an ordinary house, you have to find an extraordinary house," he explains. "This one, having a total of 30 rooms, I thought would be big enough. But I was wrong."

UPDATE: "Hesper" and "Little Luther" are no longer a part of the Wiscasset landscape. They were removed from the Sheepscot River in 1998. Before their departure, residents were permitted to pick over the ships for souvenirs. Though the bulk of the hulls went into the town's landfill, one enterprising Mainer acquired large pieces of the ship to refurbish into mementos for the tourist trade.

Good ol' Red's Eats is still going strong from April until October, with lobster rolls remaining a bargain at $11. The Musical Wonder House also remains open to visitors, from May through October, at 18 High Street (207) 882–7163 or (800) 336–3725.

MOUNT KEARSAGE
at WORK

The summit of New Hampshire's Mount Kearsage offers striking views of both the White Mountains and Vermont's Green Mountains, with a tapestry of foliage that is a magnet for tourists. In fact, tourism is the economic mainstay here. But still remembered— and cherished—are the hard work and comforting rhythms of the region's farming life.

Labors of Love

Some 200 years ago, New Hampshire farmers made a habit of reading the winds for clues to the weather. Autumn sounded the alarm to mow the fields and cut the great stacks of wood needed to get through the winter.

The rituals of New Hampshire farm life are remembered well by author Donald Hall, who lives in the Wilmot farmhouse where his mother grew up.

As a boy, Hall developed an affection not only for this place, but for the habits he observed. His reflections on those times are found in his book, *Life Work.*

"My mother, who never had a profession, has an attitude towards work very much like mine—get things done," Hall says. "She's 90 now. A letter from her might begin by saying, 'I wrote four letters today, paid my bills, and then talked to so-and-so,' listing what she had done in the day and feeling satisfied because she had filled her day with something. And I certainly feel like that, although what I am doing is rather different."

What Hall is doing is writing. Seven days a week, in the room where he slept as a boy. He has published prize-winning volumes of poetry, essays, children's books, and criticism. Hall claims that he is not disciplined. He says that it is a love for his work that brings him to his desk by 5:00 in the morning. And, he adds, it's his belief that absorption in work is the source of true contentment.

Wooly Comfort

It appears Julie Morse feels the same way. In her farmhouse in Wilmot, at the base of Kearsage, Morse spins wool from the sheep that she and her husband raise. It is work that farm women of New Hampshire once did of necessity. But, for Julie, the rhythm of the wheel and the texture of the fleece make the job a pleasure, not a chore.

"I can send my wool that's just been shorn to the wool mill, and they will wash it and comb it for me, so I can skip all that work if I want to," Julie says. "Frankly, though, I like to do it on my own, because I raise the sheep myself and I like to feel and touch the fibers. When it's work that you love, you don't think of it as work."

Although she seems to love her sheep like pets, this is no hobby for Julie. It is a business. The sheeps' wool,

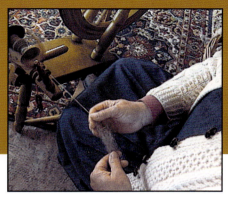

Julie Morse and friends. No animals are harmed in the spinning of wool into yarn!

and sometimes their meat, are sold in her shop, the Farm Mountain Sheep and Wool Company.

While heading over to the barn, Julie points out Alice, who is—of course—a white rabbit.

Julie's specialty product is wool from angora rabbits, which she plucks and spins. She reveals that angora is eight times warmer than sheep's wool. And she insists that being sheared is not uncomfortable for her brood. "They love it. Do these look like abused rabbits?" Julie asks with a grin.

For Julie, contentment derives not only from work, but from where that work takes place. Mount Kearsage stands at her door, and her feeling for the place is as tender as her love for her animals. "That is our mountain, and I don't know how I could live without a mountain in my face at this point. We all cherish the mountain."

Donald Hall seconds the emotion. "I have never lived anywhere where I felt such enthusiasm for place, as I do in this place," he declares. "Love of the mountain. Love of the fall. Love of the good weather. The sense of joy in the land," he exclaims. "And this also applies to people who are not like me—not making paragraphs about it and selling it to magazines. These people just live in it and love the air that they breathe."

Handmade Walls

Hall is describing people like Charlie Duncan. Duncan stands in the middle of a field on this blustery afternoon, searching for the raw material he needs for his work: fat, gray stones pried from these fields by farmers some 200 years ago.

Charlie is a builder of stone walls. Unlike some of the old farmers, who randomly piled their stones, Charlie makes his selections as carefully as Donald Hall chooses words for a poem.

Pointing to a stone with a fairly flat side to it, he announces, "This would be what I call a face—what would be exposed. And this would be a bed joint." He reaches for a second stone. "This could make a top where another rock could sit on it pretty good."

The reward of careful choice is strength, and eloquence. Using no mortar, Charlie Duncan places stone upon stone, building a testament to his craft. As a tribute to his work, he received an award from the New Hampshire Landscape Association. While he appreciates the award, he explains that his gratification comes from the task at hand, and being able to lose himself in it.

"There's more of a satisfaction than just a paycheck every week," Duncan says. "I like the feeling of organiz-

Mason Charlie Duncan

ing something out of chaos, and I like the feeling that it's going to be there for a while. Hopefully, it should last generations."

Although they shift and settle, stone walls endure. Everywhere, there are remnants from a time when this land was the domain of farmers. But more than just agricultural artifacts, these remnants are evidence of a place that was loved, owing—at least in part—to work, well done.

Home At Last

More than a century ago, Donald Hall's great-grandfather grew up on Eagle Pond Farm in New Hampshire. He left the farm when he married Hall's grandmother, Kate, and moved just down the road, into the house where Hall lives today. Hall maintains that his grandfather imparted not only his respect for work, but also an appreciation for language.

"His joy in language was in the stories he told. He milked twice a day, and I'd go up to the old tie-up in the barn where he was milking, and he would entertain me in all sorts

Kearsage has been described as a "friendly" mountain. It's an easy hike for casual climbers and is also accessible by car. One road leads to a parking lot and picnic area; from there, it's a short walk to the summit. You can reach Mount Kearsage from Winslow State Park off Route 11, three miles south of Wilmot, and from Rollins State Park off Route 103, four miles north of Warner.

of ways," Hall recalls. "He would tell me stories, he would tease me and ask me questions, full of love, always. And he would also recite poems. So this is one way that poetry came into my life. There were several ways, but this was a big way."

Hall grew up in suburban Connecticut. It was during summer vacations that he formed his attachment to the house here, and to the farm surrounding Eagle Pond. "When I was maybe 15 or 16, I thought maybe I could be a writer and live here, by my living. But then I got sensible," Hall chuckles. "I realized there was no way I could make a living as a writer, so no way I could live here. I gave it up."

Hall left New England in the late 1950s to become a professor at the University of Michigan. But he returned to the farm 18 years later with his wife, poet Jane Kenyon. After they arrived, Hall's grandmother died. Soon after, Hall and Kenyon decided to stay.

"For me, there was sudden resuscitation. Something I had dreamed of as a child, something I'd dreamed

Donald Hall, left, writing and at rest at home, center.

of for many years, had come back in full flower. And it was bliss."

Hall and his wife began to attend the tiny church in South Danbury where his grandmother had played the organ for 78 years. He says they were touched by the community, and enriched by reconnecting to the past.

Donald Hall's work was interrupted in 1992 when, halfway through the draft of his book, *Life Work*, he was diagnosed with cancer. The cancer was removed but Hall was told that his odds for living more than a few years were not favorable. "It's depressing to feel ill. It's depressing to have chemotherapy and so on, but it's not depressing to be me at this moment. I am in a good patch right now. I feel good, I have a lot of energy," he states. "I know that this won't go on terribly long, but I don't get into a panic about that or brood about it. What a waste of time. The moment is more precious than ever, and I'm more capable now of living in the pres-

At the time of our visit, there was plenty of activity on Mount Kearsage. The state of New Hampshire was cutting selected red oak trees from the mountainside as a special gift to the U.S. Navy. The wood was used to create "plankowner plaques," helping to commission the U.S.S. Kearsage. In this longstanding Navy tradition, members of a new ship receive the plaques as a symbolic piece of their ship. The original U.S.S. Kearsage was a sloop-of-war, built of Mount Kearsage red oak at the Portsmouth Naval Shipyard in 1861. The Kearsage is remembered for its victory over the Confederate cruiser, The Alabama.

ent and enjoying myself."

Hall says that living in the moment is easier for him in New Hampshire. It's an idea that he expresses in his essay, *Here at Eagle Pond*: "It turns out that the fulfillment of desire is to stop desiring. To live in the full moon and the snow, in the direction the wind comes from. In the animal scent of the alive second."

Summa Cum Supernatural

New London is the largest town in the shadow of Mount Kearsage. The neat clapboard building on the town's Main Street is easy to mistake for a church. Locals know that this is the Academy Building, used as a guesthouse by New London's Colby-Sawyer College. Inside hang portraits of the Academy's benefactors. But some suggest their presence here isn't limited to paint on canvas.

Patrick Anderson, chairman of the Department of

Patrick Anderson, telling Mary about his scary night.

Humanities, remembers his stay here all too well. Anderson was interviewing for a job at the college and, on this particular Sunday, he was the only guest in the house. Several times that day, he noticed, the door to an empty bedroom, across from his room, would be closed when he left the building, and opened when he returned. It annoyed him. So, before he went out for the evening, he locked the door, made sure that it was secure, and turned on several lights. When he returned at 11:00 that night, the lights were off and once again, the door to the room was opened.

"I was really freaked at that point," Anderson recalls. "I grabbed the door, slammed it, and walked into my room, slammed the door and dragged the dresser in front of it. That's when the spooky stuff really started happening. I was there maybe an hour when I heard footsteps. Then the sound of water started, as though someone was bathing. I knew I was alone in the building. I had confirmed that. I had checked everything else," he went on. "And the sounds of water continued for quite some time through the evening. It sounded like it was coming from across the hall, from the mysterious room where the door kept opening."

Could founder Anthony Colby be teasing his guests? Might Madam Colby's spirit be delighting in a hot bath?

UPDATE: Although Julie Morse still runs the Farm Mountain Sheep and Wool Company with her partners, she no longer raises sheep or rabbits. She is, however, still in the business of farming; she and her son now raise elk on the family's 200-acre property. Elk meat, Morse tells us, is mild and lean. And velvet from elk antlers—long prized in Asia as a health supplement—is gaining popularity in the United States.

As for the Academy Building in New London, there are no more overnight guests. The building now houses town offices where workers report that, during their nine-to-five shifts, the building is "disappointingly unhaunted." Apparently, the spirit has moved on to other quarters, possibly the library, where a woman who did overnight cleaning had an unexpected visitor—and has not been inside the library since.

Poet Donald Hall is beating the odds. Nine years after his cancer diagnosis and discouraging prognosis, he is happy to be alive and happy to be working. But shortly after our visit, Hall and his wife received news even worse than his cancer diagnosis. Jane Kenyon was diagnosed with leukemia. She died in 1995 at the age of 47. Hall's critically acclaimed collection of poetry, *Without*, examines Kenyon's death and his profound grief.

SWIFT RIVER VALLEY

In densely populated Massachusetts, is there any wilderness left? In 1986, Chronicle's Peter Mehegan traveled the state to find out. Fifty miles west of Boston, he discovered the quiet forest and clear waters of the Quabbin Reservoir. Peter also uncovered the Quabbin's hidden history—a haunting story of lost villages and fading memories.

Lost and Found

Like many Massachusetts names, *Quabbin* is a Native American word. "Meeting of the waters" is an appropriate name for this area, which is veined with rivers and streams and dominated by the reservoir, an 18-mile expanse.

The Quabbin Reservoir is a servant of many masters. It is a fine fishing ground, a wildlife sanctuary, and a photographer's heaven. But its real purpose is a bit more prosaic. Its 412 billion gallons are the water supply for all of Boston and most of eastern Massachusetts.

"It's surprising how many people don't know the Quabbin is here, and don't know this is the source of their drinking water," remarks one local resident. The Quabbin's history is even more surprising. This is not a natural lake. It is a manmade reservoir. Its creation back in the 1930s forever changed this area and the people who lived here.

"I was born and brought up here," former resident Walter King says. "I spent the first twenty-odd years of my life in the valley. I went to school here; I learned to dance here; I had my first girlfriends here; I learned to play baseball here."

One hundred years ago, several thousand people lived in the Swift River Valley, in towns whose names are all but forgotten: Prescott, Dana, Enfield, and Greenwich. This was farming country. Life was simple, quiet, and unaffected by the growing metropolis to the east. But by the end of the 1800s, Boston needed water and proposed a plan: level four towns and dam the Swift River to create a reservoir.

Locals were horrified. Some, including Walter King's father, did what they could to fight the plan. "Individually, there was not much they could do about it," King says. "My father went to Boston to attend hearings now and then, when they had them. But things didn't work out."

Eleanor Schmidt, Karen Campbell, and Walter King, remembering.

Works crews cleared the land. Bridges were blown up; houses were trucked off. In all, 3,500 residents were relocated. And it wasn't just the living who were displaced. The remains of 7,500 bodies were disinterred from 34 different cemeteries, and reburied above the Quabbin.

By July of 1939, the Winsor Dam was complete, and the Swift River began to rise. The waters covered homes, farms, churches, and schools. Today, the Quabbin "ghost towns" are gone. But the land remembers. Here and there, on land bordering the reservoir, you can still see decaying roadways and former pasture land, now covered with red pine.

Reunion

Most of the valley residents disbursed after 1939. But in the spring of our visit—nearly 50 years after they left—they have come together again.

On a sunny afternoon, the Quabbin Visitors Center is alive with quiet conversation and an occasional burst of laughter. A few dozen senior citizens sit over old photographs and warm cups of coffee. Their body language tells the story; they are sharing something of significance.

In the crowd is Karen Campbell, a center volunteer. "When we first started the Visitors Center, it became evident there were still a lot of people around who came from the valley," Campbell states. "They would come in and ask if anyone had stopped by from Prescott or Dana or the other two towns."

Campbell and her colleagues had an idea. "We decided to set aside a regular day every week so they could come and meet each other and share their memories," she explains. "Sometimes it gets pretty rowdy in here—they have some real tall tales to tell. And sometimes there are a few tears. Either way, it's great."

With photos to look at, people to remember, and stories to swap, meetings are bittersweet.

There is no going back for the people of the Swift River Valley. Their past is drowned. But, according to former Prescott resident, Eleanor Schmidt, the present holds its own magic. "I had my happiness growing up," she muses. "Nobody else has it, or can take it away." Seated on a lawn overlooking the reservoir, she adds, "I can come back here and it's still beautiful. So there is two beautiful things for me, what I had and what I've got now."

Quabbin Critters

When engineers and workers packed up their gear in 1939 after damming the Swift River and moving on, they left behind more than a reservoir. Without intending to, they had created a huge wilderness area that is now home to

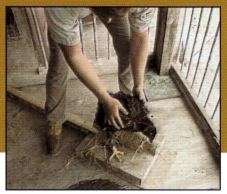

Eagle champions Paul Lyons, and Jack Swedberg.

dozens of species of wildlife. The centerpiece is the Prescott peninsula, a bustling township some 60 years ago. Today, it is off limits to virtually all human activity.

Paul Lyons is the resident wildlife biologist. "Every so often in my work, I come across an old homestead," Lyons says. "You see the stone walls, the old cellar hole. It makes you stop in your tracks, and you really appreciate what they gave up."

Re-creating a wilderness can be a satisfying yet painful process. Just ask Jack Swedberg, who's leading the effort to return bald eagles to the Quabbin.

"We went up to Nova Scotia and took eight nestling birds, and we brought them down today," Swedberg reports. "We left Sydney at 9:30 this morning and here we are. The birds are in the tower and it's 2:30 in the afternoon. So it's a great day."

Swedberg has high hopes for these eagles. "When they are ready to fledge, and after they do fledge, is when they imprint to this area as home. Then hopefully, if everything works out, they will probably go off on long flights. And I mean *long* flights. Mississippi, California, or wherever," he explains. "But when they're five years old and they're ready to breed, they come into their adult plumage. Theoretically, if everything works out properly, they will return to this area."

It has been 100 years since bald eagles last nested in Massachusetts. But within the next five years, Swedberg looks forward to seeing a nest here.

UPDATE: Jack Swedberg's Eagle Restoration Project is a story with a happy ending. In fact, the program was so successful that it put itself out of business; there's no longer a need to restore eagles in the state.

Five pairs have established their territory at the Quabbin, and their progeny have spread across the state. In all, Massachusetts is now home to eleven eagle pairs, and experts anticipate that number will only grow.

Memorabilia from the valley's lost towns is displayed at the Swift River Historical Society Museum in New Salem. The collection includes photos, records, and a former church moved to the site from the valley. The museum is open on selected days during the spring and summer months; call ahead for hours at 978–544–6882.

DOWN EAST DETERMINATION

Hard up by the Canadian border, there's a section of Maine that features rolling farm-lands and self-reliant individuals. Aroostook County is where winter makes itself known with twenty-below-zero temperatures, bone-chilling winds, a hard frost that hits in September, and a snow cover that lasts until April. We met some folks who call this place home in the winter of 1999.

The County

Snow doesn't just fall in Maine's Aroostook County. It stampedes, constantly changing the landscape, like a white tablecloth flung again and again by a fussy housekeeper.

The people who live in the Aroostook communities of Caribou, Van Buren, and Fort Kent are the kind who don't waste words. Ask them where they live, and they'll simply reply, "The County." Ask them why they live in such a place, and they'll turn adversity into advantage. If you say, "It's awfully desolate," they'll say, "It's very peaceful here."

That's what Steve Kennedy claims, although his idea of peace does not include quiet. Steve and his wife, Cathy, share their home with 30 Alaskan Husky sled dogs. In Cathy's opinion, living next door to the middle of nowhere is a perfect location. "You make all the noise you want and it doesn't bother anybody," Cathy states.

Steve and Cathy Kennedy

The Kennedys bought their first dog in 1976. A couple of years later, they decided to move to a place where they could dog sled. You get the feeling they won't be moving again. "We've lived in cities for a long time," Steve reports, "went to school in cities, and they're fine to visit, but I'd rather live out in the country."

For money, Steve commutes 13 miles north to teach music at the Fort Kent Elementary School. For passion, he mushes.

"It's exhilarating," he exclaims. "You've got something that you've got a hold of, you've got control of it, sort of—only as much as the dogs are willing to give you—and they give it to you because they love you and you've trained them and you're pretty darn lucky."

For Cathy, it's more about seizing the day along with the dogs. "You get to be really old and you can look back on your life with regrets or you can say, 'Yeah, I did that, that was pretty cool'; and that's what we're trying to do."

Alban Bouchard making ployes.

A Product from the Past

Winter freezes the ground three feet thick in "The County." That can make working the land a tricky proposition. A few years ago, a long-time farming family, the Bouchards, thought they had reached the end of the line after more than a century-and-a-half. Then they found a future, by looking back to a product from Alban Bouchard's past: ployes.

"Ployes is the bread, it's a griddle bread," he instructs. "We were raised with ployes." Ployes (rhymes with boys) is a flat bread pancake made from buckwheat, according to an old French Acadian recipe. Bouchard remembers it as a local staple, one that began to disappear with the demise of the small family farm.

"When the farms started dwindling down, the farmers started dropping by the side of the road," he laments. "There was less buckwheat that was grown, to the point where there was no buckwheat grown because there was no demand for it."

The Bouchards decided to create the demand themselves. They planted buckwheat, and turned part of their potato farm into an instant ployes plant. The gamble has paid off; today they sell their pancake mix in retail stores, by mail order, and on the Web. It's an enterprise that involves the whole family, including the patriarch, who had hoped to be winding down at his age.

"I'm 72 and I'd like to take it easy a little," Alban admits. "But I have to say I work harder now than I ever did before." But talk a little longer, and you come to realize that Alban Bouchard may not be the retiring type.

"We were born here," he says. "I remember when the winters went to weeks with 40 degrees below zero, with 40- or 50-mile-an-hour winds and 5 feet of snow." Would he rather live somewhere warm? "A lot of people go to Florida," Alban muses. "I've been to Florida. I like to be there four or five days. Then I want to come back."

The County Cure-all

The open space and chill beauty of "The County" has made it a destination for snowmobilers and others who appreciate nature in the wild. But businesses have not always found the area as attractive. Loring Air Force Base, the biggest employer in the county, shut down in 1997, making a fragile economy that much more vulnerable. For many people here, making it means making it up as you go along, with creative self-employment.

Butch Tobin, of Mapleton, is pinning his hopes on a pair of antlers. Well, actually, many pairs of antlers. Tobin

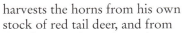
Velvet Antler fans Rodney Weeks (left) and Butch Tobin (right).

harvests the horns from his own stock of red tail deer, and from deer farmers throughout the world. He then grinds the antlers into a powder that he puts into a pill, and sells under the name Velvet Antler. The result, he claims, is a remedy for a whole raft of ailments.

"It improves circulation, improves lung efficiency," he enumerates. "It's good for lupus, fibromalgia, osteoarthritis, osteoporosis, migraine headaches, varicose veins."

And did he mention . . . "Arthritis, high blood pressure, high cholesterol, kidney and liver problems."

Tobin says the Chinese and Koreans have used the substance as medicine for centuries. In the West, though, there is no such tradition. "It's been a struggle," Tobin says, "we have a product that no one here in our part of the world has ever heard of, even though it's 2,000 years old."

Fortunately, Tobin's neighbors have heard of Velvet Antler. Several of them contributed testimonials to the Tobin Farms Web site. Eighty-one-year-old Rodney Weeks says he suffered from a chronic stiff neck until Butch slipped him some pills.

"I suppose it was arthritis maybe. It hurt when I turned my head." He demonstrates by rotating his shoulders stiffly, like Frankenstein. "After I'd been taking the capsules for about two weeks, it didn't hurt anymore," he states.

The Food and Drug Administration approaches the matter with a little more skepticism. An FDA spokesperson says it has no proof that Velvet Antler eases any of the conditions cited by Tobin; at the same time, it's had no complaints of harm from consumers.

Pickles, Please

In the town of Easton, we met another man working for a cure. Mike Henderson's miracle substance is a more traditional one: vinegar. And his ambitions are a little less bold: he's trying to spice up lunch. Henderson makes and markets "Mike's Pickles."

"I kind of did it on a whim one summer," he explains. "I had a chance to make a whole mess of pickles from my garden and what I basically did was put them all up and then somebody said, 'Can I buy some from you?'"

The former schoolteacher relished the idea of going from pupils to pickles full time. He usually makes about 14 varieties. The most popular: the chopped mustard pickle, which Mike says was personally certified by a campaigning Governor Angus King as his favorite.

Mike Henderson, left, and John Desjardins, far right.

Getting a Handle

Pickles to liven up a meal, Velvet Antler to ease an ill. These two small businesses aim to make life a little better. A larger Aroostook County employer bets on things getting worse. Smith and Wesson, the Springfield, Massachusetts, gun company, produces handcuffs at a plant in Houlton, on the last exit off I-95 before Canada. Most people don't give a lot of thought to who makes leg irons and shackles, but Smith and Wesson's Terry Wade urges the public to look for the local label.

"Every handcuff that's made in Houlton, Maine, has Houlton, Maine stamped on the back," Wade discloses. "So my people, myself, we're proud that we're the only maker of the Smith and Wesson handcuff."

The plant, which opened in 1966, employs 90 locals and cranked out its three-millionth pair of cuffs shortly before Chronicle visited. Wade says that prompted a party. "We had a big celebration and all our employees got a t-shirt and handcuffs with our name on it."

Leaving Houlton, you can't help but hope that you never see Terry Wade's handiwork in action. Freedom sounds more appealing after an introductory course in shackles.

Bicycle Bonanza

An hour north of Houlton, in Van Buren, we found a company called Aegis Bicycles, where the call of the open road gets answered. Aegis makes road bikes and mountain bikes from a plastic called carbon fiber. The company claims this is as strong as metal, but lighter, so it delivers less road shock, more responsiveness, and greater durability.

Today's Aegis actually began in 1971, manufacturing hollow graphite tennis racquets. By the mid-80s, competition prompted Aegis to drop out of the tennis business and jump into making bikes. At prices ranging from $1,500 to $3,000, the bikes have won a loyal following among triathletes, racers, and serious amateurs.

Aegis uses its Down East location as a selling point, proudly promoting its "Maine-Made" craftsmanship. According to Aegis's John Desjardins, too many people count "The County" out when it comes to recognizing New England's advantages.

"A lot of people don't realize there's civilization out here, that's how far north we are."

Well, now we know.

The ULTIMATE FLEA MARKET

Brimfield is a quiet, one-stoplight village in central Massachusetts. But three times a year—in May, July, and September—it's transformed into the largest flea market on the planet. Chronicle captured the scene in September of 1997.

Hunters and gatherers arrive from all around the globe. They are drawn by a collection of more than 20 different markets, featuring approximately 5,000 dealers offering everything from fine furniture to the latest collectibles.

Day One of each show is a race to the goods. Joel Schiff is a regular, and usually one of the first out of the gates, unslowed by the absence of one leg. His quest: to beat his competitors to the cast-iron cookware. His secret weapon: a very loud voice that cuts through the crowd, calling "Cast iron? Cast iron?"

Others advertise their desires for all to see, turning themselves into human want ads: "Desperately Seeking Poker Chips." "Civil War Items." "Daguerreotypes." "Carnival Knock-down Cats."

The show spreads over two miles worth of open fields, under thousands of tents, sprawled across card tables, and spilling out of trucks. Many of the shoppers come in teams, equipped with walkie-talkies, useful for comparing prices and locating each other.

Bob Cahn, also known as the Primitive Man, is there to help these seekers. The veteran dealer is a charter member of K.O.O.K.S. (Kollectors of Old Kitchen Stuff), and a purveyor of kerosene lamp holders, washboards, early apple peelers, and herb crushers. Among the stuff crammed into his camper, he finds an antique knife polisher. And inside the crowd, he finds a man from New Orleans who had always wanted one.

Gordon Reid

Father of the Fleas

You can call the late Gordon Reid the father of the Brimfield show. In 1951, he brought together a few dozen antiques dealers to exhibit their wares on his field. He died in the mid-1970s, but his legacy is carried on by his daughters Jill and Judy, otherwise known as J & J Promotions.

If a field doesn't have dealers parked on it, it's probably got cars parked on it, at rates ranging from three to six bucks a day. Don't even think about trying to get away with parking illegally. That's the quickest way to

Market regulars Joel Schiff, center, and Bob Cahn, right.

meet Dave Bell, owner of One Stop Towing. And when he takes you away, don't even try to bargain on the fee. Unlike almost everybody else in Brim-field for the fair, Dave is not interested in negotiating.

What makes Brimfield so special? Gary Sohmers, owner of Wex-Rex Collec-tibles in Framingham, Massachusetts, thinks he knows: There are a lot of attics and basements in New England. And those attics and basements are full of stuff. Brimfield empties out the attics and basements, and in the process fulfills the obsessions of collectors. Passion and profit, played out in fields of plenty.

Interested In Joining In the Fray?

Brimfield is centrally located on Route 20, between Exit 8 (Palmer) and Exit 9 (Sturbridge) of the Mass Pike.

Information is available on the Internet at www.brimfield-antiqueshow.com/. The Quaboag Valley Chamber of Commerce also publishes an official Brim-field guide. You can contact them at 413–283–2418, or QVCC, 1429 Main Street, Palmer, MA 01069. E-mail: qvcc@mail.ccsinet.net. Internet: www.quaboag.com

Bob Cahn comes by his quirkiness naturally. Before he became a dealer, he produced the Soupy Sales television show. One of his jobs was decorating the set with all manner of props. When the show went off the air, the discarded props went into his camper, and on sale at places like Brimfield.

ISLANDERS WANTED

Living on a small island requires special skills. You have to be able to cope with solitude. You also have to be comfortable with the fact that your neighbors will know almost everything about you. You can feel lonely one moment, closed in the next. Not many people can juggle those conflicting emotions, which is why island life is not for everybody. And it's also why island communities are constantly looking for new members. In the winter of 1987, the island town of Frenchboro, Maine, put out a call for the few, the brave, the hardy. Chronicle was there.

Frenchboro sits nine miles off the coast of Maine, accessible by ferry from Mount Desert Island. The trip takes just under an hour, but the effect of going from the tourist haven of Bar Harbor to the stark simplicity of Frenchboro feels like time travel.

Outsiders dictate Bar Harbor's rhythms: stressful in the summer, restorative in the winter. Frenchboro rises and falls with the tides that rule the main occupation—fishing. The social life revolves around school and church. There's no town hall, no year-round restaurant, no movie theater; until 1984, there weren't even phones. About 50 residents call the place home. About half of them answer to the name Lunt.

It was a Lunt who established the first commercial business on the island—a fish wharf—in 1822. When we visited, 71-year-old Vivian Lunt, the matriarch of the family, was busy as usual, serving as president of the historical society, church treasurer, treasurer of the local women's

group, and an organizer of the annual Lobster Festival. Not to mention that she paints in her spare time, a talent she nurtured by watching Maine Public Television. Clearly, she is not a person who finds it hard to fill the island hours.

"I like the peace and quiet of the life," Vivian says. "And I like to do the things that are available here. I like picnicking, I like hiking, I like boating, and I like just getting together. You know everybody."

Vivian followed a familiar path on Frenchboro. She had to leave the island to go to high school, on Mount Desert Island. After graduation, she worked for a while off-island. But then she fell in love with a Lunt, and came back.

Getting Away from the Grind

Town Treasurer Dan Blaszczuk came to Frenchboro from a different direction. He was living in Connecticut, chasing what he thought was the American Dream. But some-

Frenchboro residents Vivian Lunt, and Dan Blaszczuk.

thing didn't feel quite right, until he came to Frenchboro in 1980.

"I had had my fill of all those things that people say are the things that you're supposed be striving for in life, like one-upsmanship—playing the game. I'd had it," Blaszczuk recalls. "I originally came here for a two-week vacation. I extended it for a month. Then Labor Day came and I had a job and I asked someone to give me three reasons to leave. And no one could."

Frenchboro's teacher, Annie Pye, traded in a life in California for a home in a place where the winter temperatures can get well below zero. But she found another kind of warmth in Frenchboro.

"People are more than willing to help. When I don't bring my car over because of the ferry situation, somebody has got to help me get my groceries over here, get them off of the lobster boat into somebody else's truck and haul me up the hill and then help me unload it," Pye says. "You wouldn't find that in too many places, and here nobody bats an eyelash about it. I kept saying 'Thank you, Thank you, Thank you,' because to me it was such a monumental favor. But here it's just a way of life."

A Homesteading Solution

Still, even small towns like Frenchboro need people to keep them going, and without more newcomers like Pye, there is a danger that the way of life could disappear. In the late 1960s, residents took in nine foster children to keep the school going. Now, they are trying a new approach: a homesteading program, using state and federal funds, and land donated by the family of David Rockefeller. The goal is to bring in ten families who will choose to settle in Frenchboro. The first step is to fill out a ten-page application that will then be reviewed by a committee of nine islanders.

"We're looking for people who want to become part of a community," Blaszczuk explains, "people who are perhaps disillusioned with living in the big city. They obviously have to be able to support themselves. This is not, shall we say, a total freebie."

Vivian Lunt is blunt: island life isn't for everybody. "It takes a certain kind of person to live here, let's face it. You've got to like what's here," she says. "If you're a type that likes to go to a bar or to a picture every night or if you want to go partying every night, then you're not going to be happy here."

Lorena and Wyatt Beal didn't come looking for parties. They are checking out Frenchboro for a second time, weighing the pros and cons of making the move. Wyatt, a fisherman from Jonesport, likes what he has seen. "Life is

Rebecca Lunt, Danny Lunt, and April Davis, right.

more simple, I guess," he says. "It isn't so busy. You don't have the running around."

Island Life

Rebecca Lunt, chronicler of island ways for a local newspaper, details just how simple the daily routine can be, working at her crocheting while she talks. "Get up in the morning, and if it's a good day the men go off to the traps, and then the women do the housework, wash or whatever. Go to the mail when it gets here about one o'clock. Watch television in the evening . . . crochet."

Rebecca crochets with her group, Little Stitches. There's needling as well, and "gossip, a lot of gossip." But gossip can run out pretty quickly in a small place like Frenchboro. Then, it's time to go outside to see the members of the extended family, the deer that make regular visits to Rebecca's backyard, deer she has named Little Porky, Patty, Debby, and Danny.

"Let me tell you about Danny," Rebecca says. "One night I was out on the doorstep calling, and I was saying 'Danny, Danny where are you?' And Danny Lunt was walking down the road, and he says 'I'm right here.' And I thought at first it might have been the deer that answered me."

Hard work is mostly what you have in a place like Frenchboro, according to lobsterman Danny Lunt. That, and the pleasure of being your own boss. "I don't have anybody telling me when, or when not to, or what to, and what not to," Lunt says. No humans, that is, but Mother Nature can be pretty bossy. Lobstering is hostage to weather, to crustacean birth rates, and to added competition from new boats.

A Family Focus

A place with peace and quiet, dedicated to work and family, surrounded by nature: Frenchboro sounds like a good place to raise kids. It is, reports Tina Lunt, Danny's wife.

"It's free from drugs and violence and vandalism," Tina says. "Most of the kids here have freedom at the age of three, being able to go out on their own. And where else could you go and let your kids just roam at that age, knowing that they're going to be all right?"

Thirteen-year-old April Davis agrees. "I think that Frenchboro is a great place for kids to grow up. You get to go out more and play around. Over on the mainland, you're always worrying about getting killed or something, or somebody mugging you. But down here, nobody's going to hurt you or anything."

Still, April admits it is lonely being the only teenager on the island. And she says she is looking forward

A mid-winter traffic jam in Frenchboro, complete with sight-seers. . . .

to leaving Frenchboro's two-room schoolhouse for Mount Desert Island's high school, where she can spend time with kids her own age.

Dan Blaszczuk concedes there are negatives to life on Frenchboro, and any potential homesteaders need to know that. "We had one person who came out here on the Thursday ferry and when he saw the ferry leave the dock he got claustrophobia and said, 'Let me out!'" Blaszczuk remembers. "It's not always positive for people."

So will the Beals decide to take the plunge into island living? They are leaning that way, but it is up to their prospective neighbors to make the final decision, one that has to be definitive. "There can't be any dissension," Vivian Lunt explains. "Everyone has to agree that this person would be a good asset to the community."

Frenchboro's future became a little more assured when a conservation group bought two-thirds of the island in the spring of 2000. The daughter of David Rockefeller had put 900 acres up for sale, and residents feared that a resort developer might buy the parcel. But the Maine Coast Heritage Trust purchased the land with the promise of only limited development.

UPDATE: Wyatt and Lorena Beal moved to Frenchboro shortly after our story. They were still there in the winter of 2001, the only family left from the 1987 homesteaders. Wyatt is fishing; Lorena is the postmaster.

There have been some changes. Teacher Annie Pye moved off island shortly after our visit; Lorena says teachers usually last two years at the most. Vivian Lunt no longer lives on the island year-round. And April Davis, after going off island for school, is back on Frenchboro, married, with two kids of her own.

But the biggest news happened in 1988, the winter after *Chronicle's* visit. Dan Blaszczuk, the town treasurer we had interviewed, left the island around Christmas, and never returned. Authorities discovered thousands of dollars missing from the town's coffers, and a grand jury later indicted Blaszczuk for embezzlement. A former detective on the case says the money was eventually paid back, but Blaszczuk's whereabouts are still unknown, and an arrest warrant was still out for him in the spring of 2001.

The Real
GOLDEN POND

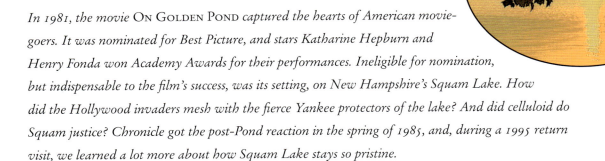

In 1981, the movie ON GOLDEN POND *captured the hearts of American movie-goers. It was nominated for Best Picture, and stars Katharine Hepburn and Henry Fonda won Academy Awards for their performances. Ineligible for nomination, but indispensable to the film's success, was its setting, on New Hampshire's Squam Lake. How did the Hollywood invaders mesh with the fierce Yankee protectors of the lake? And did celluloid do Squam justice? Chronicle got the post-Pond reaction in the spring of 1985, and, during a 1995 return visit, we learned a lot more about how Squam Lake stays so pristine.*

Squam Lake is New Hampshire's second largest lake, encompassing 7,700 acres and containing more than 60 islands, 65 miles of shoreline, and plenty of open water for boating and fishing. Sitting at the foothills of the White Mountains, it borders the towns of Sandwich, Moulton-boro, Holderness, Center Harbor, and Ashland. Some call it the last unspoiled lake in New Hampshire, and property owners there zealously guard its use.

On Golden Pond was originally a play, and it was written with Maine's Belgrade Lakes in mind, since play-wright Ernest Thompson's family had a camp there. But the film's producers decided they liked Squam better. After looking at several homes, they decided on a cottage in Holderness as the main location.

But Holderness residents weren't so sure. Natural Yankee reserve, combined with fiscal anxiety, left some people concerned about what the movie might mean for

their lake. As town historian Olive Staples puts it, "The lakes are the economic base of Holderness, and of course the whole region. And if we let the lake be polluted you just kill off the goose that laid the golden egg."

In other words, it was fine to put Squam on screen, as long as people didn't leave the theater with the idea that they could come on down. In fact, the town's leaders asked the movie makers not to list Holderness in the credits. But the secret got out anyway.

"We get more people walking through," Staples says. "They want to know where Golden Pond is. I could say 'Yes, this is where they filmed the movie' and they wouldn't know the difference."

Stargazing

Marina owner Sam Murdough got to know the stars pretty well during the filming. A dock of his served as a

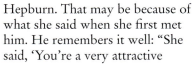

Stargazers Sam Murdough (left), and Frank Webster (right).

crucial location, and he had a house directly across from where the Fondas and Hepburn were staying. Sam's favorite of the three: Jane Fonda. She turned him into an early riser.

"You'd wake up in the morning and you'd put the binoculars on Jane's place," Murdough confesses. "She was out there on the deck doing her aerobics, and in very good shape."

If Jane was the Fonda who kick-started Sam's day, Henry was the one who helped him wind down.

"I could come home at night after work and watch Henry go out in one of my boats that he'd rented for the whole time, to go fishing, which he did almost every night," Murdough reminisces. "Henry was a super guy. He was just like my father. The kind of a person you could sit down and chat with, and you'd never know he was a star."

Katharine Hepburn, apparently, was a different story. "Katharine, I think, was more to the point where she wanted you to know she was a star," he says. "She fired several people on the movie while it was being made. She's a crusty old broad, alright."

Frank Webster has a different view of Katharine Hepburn. That may be because of what she said when she first met him. He remembers it well: "She said, 'You're a very attractive man.'" Webster warmed to the New England native immediately, perhaps recognizing a kindred spirit. "The thing I like about her is that she's just down to earth," he says. "She's just as simple as you and I are."

Now some people around Holderness explain this mutual attraction by claiming that Hepburn was just staying in character. Because if there is anyone on Squam who resembles Henry Fonda's Norman Thayer Jr., it's Frank Webster—a man described as a little cantankerous, all–New Hampshire Yankee, and slightly mischievous, especially behind the wheel of his boat, the Penguin.

At 82, Frank believes in telling it straight. So, while he liked Hepburn, the movie was something else. "I didn't like it," he admits. "It was stupid."

But Webster loves Squam. Owner of 2,700 acres, thanks to his grandfather's purchase in 1885, he still marvels at what people will pay to get onto the shoreline.

"They used to buy the stuff for two dollars a front foot," he says. "Now it's 700. Some of it's been sold for over a thousand dollars a front foot." He shakes his head. "Just to dabble your feet in the water."

Squam residents Dr. Sidney Howe (left), and John Silber (right).

The Spirit of the Northern Waters

Or to listen to the loons. The plaintive wail of those water birds is an emotional high point in *On Golden Pond,* and a daily feature on Squam Lake in spring and summer. The Cree Indians called the loon the Spirit of Northern Waters, hearing its cry as that of a dead warrior forbidden entry into heaven. But at Squam, it serves as the punctuation mark to the day.

For a long time, wildlife biologists believed that loons were monogamous, with couples staying together for as long as 30 years, giving the fictional Thayer marriage a run for its money. But the latest research removes some of that romance, revealing loon loyalty is not that legendary after all, and that, just as in the human world, mates come and go.

Loons are powerful swimmers, able to dive as deep as 200 feet, and equally adept airborne, with a flying speed up to 90 miles an hour. But they are slow and clumsy on land, making them vulnerable to predators like raccoons.

On Squam, biologists working with the Loon Preservation Committee have taken steps to protect the birds, including lashing together a raft to serve as a potential nest. The hope is that the loons will adopt the floating refuge, keeping them away from the shoreline with its predators, boats, and development.

But sometimes the loons like to pick their own accommodations. And residents, who guard the loons as fiercely as they do the lake, have adjusted. One of the biologists shares the story of an island cottage that was adopted by a nesting pair.

"About two years out of three we have a pair of loons that nest on that island. They have an alternate site elsewhere, but when they nest there, the lady that owns the island refuses to rent the camp while the loons are there. So she loses a couple of thousand dollars probably in rentals, but the loons have a safe site to nest."

Squam Squabble

Loons may get that welcome feeling, but outsiders sometimes get the impression that Squam is by invitation only. In 1995, we returned to Golden Pond and plunged into an ongoing debate about access.

Boaters are complaining about the state of the public ramp. Tourists find it hard to get a view of the lake without paying for it. Dr. Sidney Howe, a longtime land owner on the lake, argues that it is in the interest of the lake's residents to provide more public use.

"Here at Squam the problem is one of equitable access to the water surface, particularly for New Hampshire people, but also tourists, who must come to feel that

Phil Preston and others enjoying the water.

Squam is theirs to enjoy," Howe states. "Or, they're not going to support, over time, the state's conservation role in saving this unique place."

Howe points out that New Hampshire taxpayers subsidize conservation and water quality programs at Squam, even paying for stocking the fish. They should, he believes, get back something more than a feeling of virtue. But he finds himself at odds with most Squam residents. "It's pretty hard to sell this view that citizens have to share in resources in order to have their taxpayer money over time conserve them, when the majority of shore owners have been successful over the years in keeping it the way it is," Howe concedes.

The Squam Lakes Association proposes a solution: offer access to two islands for visitors and two forest preserves for day trekkers. In the view of Executive Director Phil Preston, that means that the public will be able to enjoy the lake, within reason.

"Our program is geared toward sharing this lake with whoever wants to come here," Preston insists, "although we do like to set the parameters, such as encouraging certain types of boats and not encouraging the larger boats."

Boston University's John Silber, owner of a summer place and a master of plain speaking, declares that Squam needs no changes. "It's a very nice, rustic, undeveloped looking place," Silber stresses. "No hamburger stands, no ice cream stands on the lake, and a very restful, quiet place to be. There's public access, you have several public beaches where people can put boats in."

This is clearly an emotional issue for Silber: "They can divest all the people who've owned property around here of their rights. Sure, why not—the hell with the Constitution. And what public good is accomplished? Everybody talks about diversity, well how about a little diversity by having one place that isn't Trashville! But to say the public is denied access is just plain false."

It's a quintessential New England story. How do you keep a golden place from becoming tarnished, without building walls around it? Perhaps a Hollywood screenwriter could craft an easy ending, with all parties satisfied and smiling. On Squam Lake, property owners and public advocates find they have to work a little harder to find the balance between access and preservation. But there's always cool, clear water, and the lonely cry of the loon, to remind them of what's at stake.

ONLY IN
NEW ENGLAND

FOR *the* LOVE *of* LOBSTERS

What draws tourists to the coast of Maine? Is it the dramatic shoreline? The pictur-esque harbors? The refreshing salt air? Guess again. Most visitors come for the chance to don a plastic bib, ignore all table manners, and indulge in one of the most delectable treats the ocean has to offer. In 1992, Chronicle's Peter Mehegan went in search of the allure and lore of lobsters.

Crustacean Nation

Half of all lobsters caught in New England come from Maine, and luckily for tourists, most are caught in the summertime. As the waters warm, lobsters begin roaming the ocean floor for food; some travel more than a mile-and-a-half in a day. With some six million traps off Maine's coast, there's plenty of lobster to satisfy the tourist trade. But there's also growing concern about the demise of the tasty crustacean. Still, lobsterman Steve Miller sees no reason for worry. "The biologists and the other people keeping track of this predicted record disastrous years the past two years, and each year got better," Miller says. "Of course they're predicting another disastrous year, so we're looking forward to another good year!"

Good perhaps, but never easy. Lobstering is tough work, and people choose the business for all sorts of rea-

Lobsterman Steve Miller

sons. "I heard a guy from Stonington say once that it's sort of a burning desire down in your stomach," Miller answers, when asked what keeps lobstermen going. "It makes you a little foolish, a little crazy. It makes you want to get up at 4:00 in the morning. And you do it day in and day out. You get up and you haul."

Here in the waters of Wheeler Bay near Spruce Head, there's money to be made. Miller has 1,000 traps to check this week. Though the schedule is tough, he still prefers it to life on land.

"I was ashore—for four years. I went to college for five years, and got a couple of degrees," he explains. "I went and worked in the pulp and paper industry, and I found out that if you want to go to the top of any organization, you have to work night and day. If the phone rings, you have to answer it. If you're in the middle of your kid's birthday party and something

The most unusual of the catch go to Sam Chapman at the University of Maine's marine laboratory (above).

goes wrong, you're the one they call. So after four years of that, I decided that if I wanted to be important, I might as well be important to myself."

This season, lobster prices have been as volatile as the New York Stock Exchange, ranging from a low of $3.25 per pound to a high of $7.25.

"If you've caught 100,000 pounds of lobster and they're selling at $6.00 or $7.00 a pound, well . . . $300,000 is not a bad profit for a couple of days' work," Miller acknowledges.

Next stop for Miller's catch is Art's Lobster, a wholesale dealer in Spruce Head, where the lobsters are held in large holding tanks that float in saltwater pens. "You might be able to keep lobsters alive for four days in the tanks," explains Eddie Ospland. "But when they're soft-shell, you don't want to hang onto them—you want to keep them moving. Because if they croak, nobody's going to pay for them. I learned that from experience."

Rainbow Nation

In Maine, it's illegal to keep undersized or oversized lobsters. If you land a "megalobster," you have two choices: throw it overboard, or give it to Sam Chapman of the University of Maine's marine laboratory. Pulling an enormous creature from one of the lab's many tanks, Chapman shows his expertise. "This one weighs 13 pounds, but he's not that big. I've seen 23-pounders, and a 23-pounder is going to be half again as long as this one," he says. "You routinely hear stories from lobstermen who fish these big traps—the ones that are almost two feet wide and four feet long. They tell me sometimes when they're bringing up a trap, there's a lobster that covers the whole top of the trap." If you approach a 13-pounder for a closer look, Chapman is quick with a warning: "I guarantee you, if you put your finger in that claw, your bone will be crushed." Just to prove his point, he places two large clamshells in the lobster's claws. Immediately, there is a jarring noise as the shells snap into pieces.

Over the years, Chapman has collected a remarkable assortment of mutant lobsters. One creature in his care is a lobster with a second crusher claw where a smaller ripper claw ought to be. Also in the lab are yellow lobsters, albino lobsters, and even a two-toned creature of green and orange. "These colors split right down the middle. This is one of the real strange things we get from time to time," he reports. "I don't know why this happens, but it's quite dramatic."

Chapman's most prized specimens are his blue lob-

Beth Gimbel's lobster kitsch,
and Sam Chapman's lobster chic.

sters. He's been able to breed blue males with blue females to create blue offspring. "If you look at the numbers caught off the Maine coast every year, there must be fourteen to sixteen million lobsters—maybe more. One in every three or four or five million turns out to be blue," he says. "There are probably more down there, but we don't know that for certain."

The lab's mission is to determine ways to replenish Maine's thinning lobster stock. However, Chapman can't help but wonder if, along the way, he's stumbled onto a potential goldmine. "As far as blue lobsters are concerned, the world market is untapped," he maintains. "The Japanese, I believe, favor the color blue. Maybe we could either raise these inside, or produce them for release into the wild—like the prize at the bottom of the Cracker Jack box for the lobstermen. Maybe they'd bring in eight or ten or twelve dollars a pound." Designer

jeans made a bundle in their day . . . why not designer lobsters?

Lobster "Traps"

Call it aquaculture with a subculture. True fanatics want to do more than eat lobster. They want to wear it, read about it, and play with it. The Smiling Cow gift shops, in Boothbay and Camden, are happy to oblige.

Salesperson Beth Gimbel plants her tongue firmly into her cheek and shows off the season's hottest lobster souvenirs. "These are our lobster boxer shorts, this is our lobster harmonica, and here's our trick lobster. It jumps and squeaks when you push this rubber part," she demonstrates. Also for sale are lobster windmills, lobster earrings, and even lobster literature. "This book, *Caring for Your Pet Lobster*, is a must," Gimbel insists, while moving on to one of her favorites—the lobster claw potholder. "A friend of mine used two of these as part of her Halloween costume," she says. "And here's a blow-up lobster for the kids to use at the pool or the beach.

David Jackson and his altered license plate (Maine's standard plates at far right).

And this plastic lobster is actually a water gun—the water squirts from its mouth. We also have a lobster claw fanny pincher. I'll leave that one up to your imagination."

And when in Maine, beware of lobsters by the highway. Every summer, posted signs that read "Lobster Xing" bring a few gullible motorists screeching to a halt.

Of Lobsters, Licenses, and the Law

When Maine officials selected the lobster as the official symbol for the state's license plates, most drivers heartily approved. Most, but not all.

"First of all, it's a red lobster, which is a dead lobster," motorist David Jackson points out. "The natural lobster, in its natural state, is a greenish blue. Secondly, I think a boiled lobster is a symbol of affluence, and I think that there are a lot of people in Maine who simply don't share that kind of affluence." Jackson's complaints continue. "Also, very importantly, it's representative of only a small portion of the state. After all, Maine is the Pine Tree State. If we're going to put some kind of icon on our license plates, it probably should be the pine tree, since it's more representative of all of the state."

Jackson and a small group of fellow Mainers waged a campaign to impeach the lobster. When their efforts failed, Jackson turned to civil disobedience. "This is my mild protest against the lobster plates," he explains as he shows off his personal plate. "I did a very simple thing. I got some white paint and I painted out the lobster," he reveals. "I think I did a fairly artistic job here. And I think I've produced a plate that's much more attractive than the one with the lobster on it."

The long arm of the law did not agree, however. "A policeman noticed the plate and saw that something was wrong with it. He pulled me over to take a look at it," Jackson recounts. "He asked me where the lobster was, and I said 'I painted it out.' He said, 'That's against the law.' But I was feeling a little assertive, so I said, 'The hell it is!' And that was just enough of a challenge to raise some doubts in his mind, so he let me go."

We wondered about an alternative creature to symbolize Maine—the black fly, perhaps?

"Well," answers Jackson, "there's certainly more flies here in Maine than there are lobsters!"

Cabbage Island Clambake

It's the best of Maine, all rolled into one: a scenic boat ride

A classic Cabbage Island clambake.

in Boothbay Harbor; a visit to a tiny, welcoming island; and a plentiful, old-fashioned clambake served in rustic surroundings.

The afternoon begins with the boarding of the *Argo* and a brief trip to Cabbage Island. Waiting there are members of the Moore family, who have spent all morning preparing the fixings: chowder, twin lobsters, sweet corn, potatoes, clams, and dessert. Oh, and hard-boiled eggs—they'll explain why. Jennifer Moore says the portions are so generous that only rarely does anyone ask for seconds. "Actually, we had a ten-year-old boy out here who had three lobsters and four pieces of cake, and said he was still hungry," she recalls. "But we told him he needed to diet."

Purists claim that boiling takes some of the flavor out of the lobster. But Cabbage Island's Keith Derraine says the secret is to steam it in seaweed. "The seaweed keeps all the steam in, and the steam extracts an iodine from the seaweed and goes to the food," Derraine explains. "That's one of the things that give it the taste, as well as the burning wood, and the steam itself. It's so tender when it's cooked this way, it almost melts in your mouth."

The food is steamed in layers. Vegetables on the bottom, steamers and lobster in the middle, and on top, an egg. "The egg started as a timing device for cooking," Jennifer Moore reveals. "When we stack everything—vegetables, lobsters, steamers—the egg would be on the top because it takes the shortest amount of time to cook. And so, the way everything's stacked, when the eggs are done, we know everything else is done."

Out around the picnic tables, the visitors are getting down to work. One man from

Looking for a lobster overdose? Check out the Maine Lobster Festival held annually in Rockland. For five days in August, the town goes "loco over lobsters." Among the highlights: a parade, boat rides, musical entertainment, craft shows, and, of course, thousands of pounds of lobster. Don't miss the Maine Sea Goddess Coronation Pageant, King Neptune and his Court, and the Great International Lobster Crate Race.

Maine Lobster Festival, P.O. Box 552, Rockland, Maine 04841, or call 1-800-LOB-CLAW

South Carolina is in lobster heaven. "We enjoy lobster tremendously; we never expected two of them though!" he exclaims. "We just made our way through twin lobsters last night around 9:00, and here it is 2:00 in the afternoon, and we're at it again!" His wife confirms his passion. "That's all he's talked about!" she interjects. "We've driven 1,500 miles and all he's talked about is lobster, lobster, lobster!"

But at the next table, another lobster tale tops that one. A man who hails from Indiana has been on a feeding frenzy for 11 straight days. "It started in Montreal—I started inhaling lobster there. Then we moved on to Quebec City, then around Cape Breton Island. Then down the coast, all the way through New Brunswick and Maine. Lobster every day for 11 days," he discloses. "I think they'll arrest me for eating that many lobsters. There must be something wrong with it, because it's just too good."

Watching out-of-towners eat lobster is always good for a few laughs. First-timers are often overcome with a sudden sympathy for their recently departed crustaceans. "I don't like to look at it when my husband cracks it open," admits one Midwesterner. "There's so much gunk inside. You know, lobster is a lot like liver. I love to eat liver, but I won't handle it and I won't cook it. Somebody else has to do that."

Every summer, the great tomalley debate rages: to eat or not to eat? The greenish gooey substance inside the lobster body is considered a delicacy by some, but disgusts others. One diner wrinkles her nose as she declares, "I don't like it at all. I saw green and red and it bummed me out. So you just have to scrape it off and eat the tail meat. That's the best part."

Cabbage Island has been the site of clambakes since 1956. Its name comes from the skunk cabbage that once grew here. Today, the only growth on the island is the girth of satisfied customers. "Sure, you have some doggy bags," Derraine says. "But most people just go home with a big stomach. The boat sinks down a little lower on the return trip."

To go and stuff yourself, contact Cabbage Island Clambake at P.O. Box 21, East Boothbay, ME 04544 or call 207–633–7200.

ABANDONED NEW ENGLAND

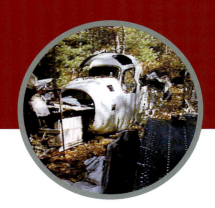

Historian William Robinson tells us that "you can trace New England's history from all that's left over." In 1991, Peter Mehegan followed Robinson's lead and uncovered tales of dreams and disaster, told in the ruins left behind.

Secrets from the Skies

Some holes in the ground are not *just* holes in the ground. Some hold secrets known to Larry Webster of Charlestown, Rhode Island. Webster, an aviation archaeologist, knows that certain holes are actually impact craters made by planes that crashed during World War II. Webster is dedicated to learning the stories behind these little-known accidents, and preserving the memories of the young pilots and crew who never returned.

"During World War II, we had a great increase in technology," Webster explains. "We had young fellows who had grown up on the farms of the Midwest suddenly learning to fly aircraft with 200 horsepower engines that fly 400 miles per hour. These were 18-, 19-, 20-year-old young men. The people who maintained the aircraft also were just kids. Instead of maintaining their cars, they had aircraft to work on."

It's not hard to see how

Larry Webster, aviation archaeologist.

mistakes were made. "We had accidents from mechanical error, from pilot error, and from the weather, which can be quite bad here in New England," Webster says.

Webster has investigated more than 300 crash sites throughout New England over the span of 20 years. Chronicle joined him on one of his expeditions into the woods of Rhode Island.

"It's pretty obvious that this is where the aircraft crashed," Webster explains, standing over a large depression in the ground. "The crater dug from the impact is 20 to 25 feet in diameter." Then he adds a surprise. "The pilot who flew this aircraft is still alive today," Webster says, "but he doesn't want to acknowledge the accident."

A visit to Webster's backyard is like a tour of a Steven Spielberg backlot. Lost aircraft from World War II reappear, exhumed from their graves. Webster points out the remains of a Hellcat, as well as the

The Hansel and Gretel Forest, then and now.

plane that hit it. He also found one plane that crashed with its wings folded.

Webster is trying to compile a list of every aviation accident that ever occurred in New England. "It's always bothered me that on, for example, Veterans Day, there's been no mention of these losses locally," he explains. "We honor the men who were lost overseas, but nobody is particularly aware of the individuals who died in these local hometowns throughout New England."

Surrounded by reminders of disaster and tragedy, it's not surprising that Webster has never had the urge to fly. "I decided it was more fun to dig than to fly," he admits. "Besides, I don't want to be the last entry on my own list!"

Fairy Tale Forest

Arthur Palme was a noted environmentalist known by his followers as the "dean" of Berkshire photographers. Palme photographed many western Massachusetts landscapes until his death in 1949. In a retrospective book, he left a curious image from the past: a bizarre stand of truncated, twisted trees known as the Hansel and Gretel Forest. He wrote that the trees were located in the Savoy

State Forest in Savoy, Massachusetts, but said they were "practically inaccessible."

Though Palme took the photo more than half a century ago, curiosity got the better of us. Chronicle's Peter Mehegan decided to find out if the Hansel and Gretel Forest still exists.

Back in the 1930s, the Civilian Conservation Corps built roads, trails, dams, and log cabins in the Savoy Mountain State Forest. The camps they set up can still be rented to this day.

The Corps also planted a large stand of white pine near Border Mountain. It was nature that turned these trees into the Hansel and Gretel Forest. "An ice storm laid these trees down," Forest and Park Supervisor David Wood reveals. "Broken pieces of large trees crushed the smaller trees. Eventually the broken pieces decomposed, but the trees underneath were permanently crooked after that. Some even had a series of bends."

Wood becomes thoughtful as he speculates that the progression of nature will soon prevail: "My guess would be that in not too many more years there won't be a crooked forest here," he predicts. "They'll all be fallen down."

Carl Byron and the ruins of the Grand Trunk Southern line.

The Train that Went Down with the Titanic

New England is crisscrossed by abandoned rail lines. Carl Byron has followed these routes since he was a child. Today, Byron is president of the Boston and Maine Railroad Historical Society, and knows his history well.

"One of the great dreams that never happened was construction of the so-called Grand Trunk Southern Line," Byron declares. "The area was pretty much covered by railroads as it was—railroads that had a great deal of political clout. So Central Vermont interests, under owner Charles Hayes, had a rough row to hoe to compete with these people."

Although workers did manage to complete a fair amount of earthwork on the line, tragedy struck when Mr. Hayes chose to return from a trip to England on the Titanic. With his death, the railroad plans fell into disarray. "The ruins—still visible along the Massachusetts turnpike and across southern New England—are the end of Hayes's dream," Byron says.

UPDATE: Larry Webster has been one busy man since our visit. He is one of the founders of the new Quonset Air Museum, located on the former Quonset Point Naval Air Station in North Kingston, Rhode Island. Webster fields a number of calls every year from sons and daughters of World War II veterans who are in search of family history.

◆

And, all these years later, "you can still see the crooked forest," reports Savoy Forest and Park Supervisor Tim Zelazo. "You just have to look *up*—after all, the trees have grown now." Zelazo adds that he has doubts about the story of the ice storm, and wonders whether it was man, not nature, that created the crooked forest. "With Bannis Road so nearby, you have to wonder whether someone just walked into the forest and decided to cut away at the trees."

SUMMER CAMPS
for GROWNUPS

Whoever said "youth is wasted on the young" may well have said the same thing about summer camp. But times are changing. Thousands of adults, from singles to seniors, are discovering that camp isn't just for kids anymore. And they're making those discoveries right here in New England. Chronicle visited a few adult camps in 1994.

Putting on the Dog

Welcome to Vermont's "Camp Gone to the Dogs," a week's worth of four-legged fun for 220 human campers and 350 dogs. CGD's founder and director Honey Loring says campers and their canines come from as far away as California.

Seated on an Adirondack chair on a wide expanse of lawn, Loring surveys the scene. "Don't you find it remarkably clean around here?" she asks. "We're taking care of things," she points out. "Camp started off with 23,000 poop bags."

Loring explains that the people who come to dog camp "are not your *average* dog people." She doesn't need to elaborate. Doggie softball games (better known as "slimeball"), obstacle courses, costume parades, training, lectures, *and* a course in dog paddling are all included in the fee, which ranges from $800 to $1,200 per

Honey Loring and friends.

week. Lectures can get quite serious at times. When Chronicle visited, we dropped in on one entitled "The Overly Bonded Human," but skipped "Puppy Kindergarten."

CGD has plenty of repeat campers. "I think my dogs remember," one camper confides, as she plays doggie catch in the pond. "When I drive up the road, they know where they are; they start barking, their tails are going like mad. Look at this place—it's total dog fun!"

Another camper displays his love for his Malamute with a brand new Malamute tattoo on his shoulder. "I went to the tattoo parlor right here, when I was in camp," he reveals, admitting, "when it was done, my dog wasn't really very impressed."

Another camper, cradling a pair of Pekinese dressed in cowboy hats, highlights one of the major benefits of CGD: "You don't have to be

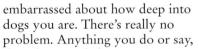
*AMC's Rob Burbank
and campers.*

embarrassed about how deep into dogs you are. There's really no problem. Anything you do or say, the other people here get it." (You can get it too, via www.campgonetothedogs.com or 802–387–5673.)

Family Affair

At the Appalachian Mountain Club's Elder Hostel camp there are adults and children who are related to each other, but no parents. That's because this weeklong camp, located at the foot of New Hampshire's Mount Washington, is exclusively for grandparents and their grandchildren. They come to the White Mountains for hiking, for natural history, and for togetherness.

The first order of business is to work out bunk arrangements. For the Younger family of Tennessee, that means Grandma and Grandpa share a pair of bunk beds with their two grandsons. You guessed it—the kids get the top bunks.

John and Bunny Nutter of Massachusetts are here with their grandson Jamie. John had hiked these mountains as a child. "We wanted to give Jamie the same start that we had," he explains. "I remember my first hike with my father. There was a farmer with us who lived in the area, a very active fellow. He was around the same age I am now—77. He went on and climbed Mount Chocurua, and I thought he was as old as Methuselah!"

The AMC's Rob Burbank explains that the program is designed for active elders. "As with all elder hostel programs, they're geared toward older people who want to get out and they want to learn something," Burbank says. "That's what I love about it; they really want to learn!"

Days here are filled with hikes and instruction in outdoor skills. Nights are spent around the campfire, with songs, stories, and a generous supply of toasted marshmallows. But, with bedtime comes a terror known to campers around the world. "Just one question," Chronicle's Mary Richardson delicately asks the Youngers. "With four people in one room, does anybody here snore?" It doesn't take long for the grandsons to answer "Yes!" in unison.

Mary decides to press on, asking the boys if they will reveal names. Without hesitation, they point the finger at their granddad.

But when Mary turns to Mr. Younger for confirmation, he deftly answers, "My wife tells me I do, but *I've*

never heard me snore!" (For information on this and other Elder Hostel programs, call 877–426–8056 or visit www.elderhostel.org.)

Hookers Welcome

Sunapee, New Hampshire, is home to a country inn unlike any other. This particular inn is chock full of *hookers*. Here tantalizing tidbits of conversation float over the front lawn, such as one guest commenting to another: "You have an excellent technique!"

Yes, the Dexter Inn, best known for its tennis, swimming, and gourmet meals, opens its doors twice a year to a summer camp of 40 rug hookers. The camp is run by "Madam" Betty Maley, who says hers may not be the oldest profession, but it comes darn close. "Rug hooking goes back to the Egyptians, if you trace it back through history, and then to the Vikings," Maley claims.

Some campers make small, decorative pieces. Others screw up their courage to take on rugs of Himalayan proportions. One hooker chooses a 9-by-12-foot challenge. "I'd like to get it done in at least two years," she says, hopefully. "If you saw me three weeks ago, when I started

it, I almost had heart failure, I was so afraid of it. But I've moved into it and it's okay now."

In earlier times, hooking was no idle hobby. "It was a means of economics," Maley explains. "People needed floor coverings, so they made rugs out of their old, used clothing. Some of the rugs were made with Grandpa's red flannel long johns! But if you're a lazy hooker like I am, you buy the wool new."

UPDATE: Since our visit, the "hookers" have picked up their rugs and moved camp to the New London Inn in New London, New Hampshire. To hook up with more information, contact the hooker's newest "madam" at 908–757–5257.

QUIRKY COLLECTIONS

Bottles. License plates. Old tools. You name it—there's probably a New Englander who collects it. Why do we hold onto these things? Yankee magazine editor Jud Hale has an answer. "We're pack rats. Look at me! Look at my desk!"

Surveying the jumble of junk on and around his desk, we realize Hale has a point. Many of New England's unusual museum collections grow out of someone's desk drawers, living room, or the need to share a chapter in history that deserves remembering. Chronicle set out to explore some of the oddest museums in New England. They may not be on a par with the Smithsonian or the Louvre, but what they have—in excess—is personality.

Heavy Metal

In Worcester, Massachusetts, of all places, the Medieval Age is alive and well. Standing like a castle atop a Worcester hill is the Higgins Armory Museum, built by a man who was captivated by the romance and craftsmanship of the Middle Ages.

"The Higgins Armory is unique in the nation," boasts director Joseph Schwarzer. "It's the only museum dedicated to the study of arms and armor, and that makes it very special indeed. If you go to some of the major collections in the United States, you'll find that they invariably present these pieces as art objects, which is a facet of what they are. But they are also historical indices," Schwarzer adds. "They were there when history was being *made*."

John Woodman Higgins of Worcester grew up enchanted by the tales of knights and knighthood. Later in life, as president of the Worcester Pressed Steel Company, he marveled at the artistry and craftsmanship of early armor and began collecting it. By the 1920s, Higgins realized that his home could no longer accommodate his ever-expanding collection. He decided to build a museum that would serve as a showcase for the art of metal working, with armor as the focus.

When Higgins opened his collection to the public, his desire to share his appreciation of armor and steel work was fulfilled. But his passion for collecting never stopped. Through the Great Depression and after World War II, Higgins filled the museum's Great Hall with more than 100 of the finest pieces of armor in the western hemi-

At the Higgins Armory Museum, Worcester, Massachusetts.

sphere. Many pieces were purchased in 1941 from newspaper legend William Randolph Hearst. Museum curator Walter Karcheski says it was a Hearst "yard sale" of sorts. "Hearst was starting to sell off things during the Depression," Karcheski explains. "He found that he wasn't selling as much or as quickly as he thought he would. So in 1941, he had the entire fifth floor of Gimbel's Department Store cleared out, and they price-tagged arms and armor elements and put them up for sale."

And you didn't have to be an art collector or historian to check out the goods. "We still have some photographs showing these people as if they are in Filene's Basement or something, looking over these bits and pieces of armor," Karcheski chuckles.

As a youngster growing up in the neighborhood, Karcheski used to trick-or-treat at Higgins's home. Once the museum opened, his frequent visits turned into a full-time passion for history.

The Armory is a museum for everyone, but children are often the most enthusiastic visitors. During a hands-on demonstration, program manager Doug Cosby gives kids a chance to try history on for size.

Cosby slides a helmet over the head of a young volunteer, then addresses his wide-eyed audience. "The suit

of armor would be made for an individual," he tells them. "You would go to an armorer and be measured for a suit, just like you would be measured for a suit of clothing today. And the suit was designed to fit like a second skin, very close to the body."

Cosby turns back to his volunteer. "Is it getting hot in there?"

"No," comes the answer.

"No? Well, it will!" With that, Cosby snaps shut the helmet's faceplate, drawing laughter and excitement from the audience.

Meanwhile, in the Quest Gallery, visitors get a chance to suit up as King Arthur or dress as Maid Marian. Most lose all inhibition and indulge in the fantasy. The young "maidens" raise the question of whether the women of the time also wore armor.

"Probably the most famous woman to wear armor was, of course, Joan of Arc," Karcheski answers. "Joan wore armor from about 1429 until 1431, when she was of course captured by the Burgundians, turned over to the English, and executed as a witch—at the age of 19!"

Most of the armor in the collection appears to be in perfect condition. It makes you wonder why you never see the marks of battle. "Sometimes you do see dents,"

P.T. Barnum and his museum, Bridgeport, Connecticut. At far right, museum director Linda Altschuler.

Karcheski says. "More often than not, though, like with your car, you do some maintenance afterwards. If you've driven on a long trip, you make sure your radiator is filled and the oil and so forth. With the armor, any damaged pieces would be repaired right away. Because if it's weakened, then it's a vulnerable spot the next time you go into combat."

Even man's best friend received special treatment. As proof, there's a full suit of armor for the Museum's canine mascot, "Helmutt."

When he died in 1961, John Woodman Higgins left his collection intact for the public to enjoy. "This is not only a national resource," Karcheski emphasizes, "but it's something that was born and bred in Worcester. There just isn't anything else like this." (For more information, try www.higgins.org or call 508–853–6015.)

One Born Every Minute

Inside a stately building in Bridgeport, Connecticut is a museum celebrating the life and times of Phineas Taylor Barnum. It's a fitting tribute to a man who single-handedly founded two museums of his own in New York City before organizing his first circus.

The Fiji Mermaid

Barnum, it's been said, was a mix of Ted Turner, Walt Disney, and Donald Trump, all rolled into one remarkable promoter. "He understood audiences," explains museum director Linda Altschuler. "He took things that already existed, and re-invented them. He took the circus, and turned it into three rings. He made Jenny Lind the biggest singer in America. He made things bigger, brighter, and better, and was able to sell it to an audience that loved every minute of it."

Among Barnum's most successful exhibits was the Fiji Mermaid. This scam—half-monkey and half-fish—fooled thousands and made Barnum a rich man.

Another display details the story of General Tom Thumb, and the many other "little people" employed by Barnum. Altschuler points out a tiny version of Cinderella's coach. Instead of a pumpkin-shaped carriage, this one resembles a walnut. "This wonderful miniature carriage was built for Commodore Nutt, who was one of the many 'little people' to accompany Tom Thumb," she reports. "And over here is a mural depicting Tom Thumb, his wife Lavinia Warren, her sister, Minnie, and Commodore Nutt. This was Tom and Lavinia's wedding, with 2,000 people attending, at Grace Church in New York City."

  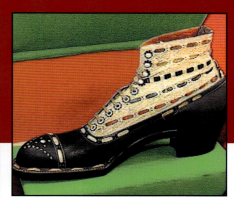

Fancy footwear at the Brockton Shoe Museum, Brockton, Massachusetts.

On the museum's third floor is a scale model of a five-ring tent. Measuring 1,000 square feet and adorned with miniature animals, performers, cages, and rings, the model depicts every detail of circus life.

"Barnum was kind of a Renaissance man of the 19th century," Altschuler states, "but he's primarily known for the circus, and for loving to pull humbugs on people." (For museum hours call 203–331–1104.)

These Shoes Are Made for Gawking

Despite rumors to the contrary, Imelda Marcos is not a charter member of the Brockton Shoe Museum in Brockton, Massachusetts. The museum came to be when shoe manufacturer William Doyle donated his private collection to the Brockton Historical Society.

Resident sole man John Learned, the president of Brockton's Historical Society, is happy to show off the celebrity shoe exhibit. "Very recently, we received these jogging shoes from President Clinton. Size 13, Nike Swish shoes. And here's another one of our treasures. Arthur Fiedler's formal pumps. He wore them for his performances as conductor of the Pops."

Shoes of Ted Williams, Jay Leno, Marvin Hagler, Rocky Marciano—they're all here. And the biggest ones of all? Size 24 shoes worn by Primo Carnera, a one-time world heavyweight boxing champion.

"We also have a very extensive military footwear collection," adds Learned, "from Civil War boots through World War I, Korea, right through Desert Storm." He displays an interesting shoe called the Attenuator, designed for anti-mine protection. "It's worn over the service shoe and has a specially designed shank to divert a blast," Learned explains.

From metal-rimmed children's shoes from the Colonial era to boots that might look stylish on Mars, this is a museum for anyone looking for a lift. (To plan a visit, call the historical society at 508–583–1039.)

Bottoms Up

Ye Ol' Watering Hole, on Pleasant Street in Northhampton, Massachusetts is more than a bar—it's a beer can museum. Dino Dalmolin, a part-time bartender, serves as curator. "Probably the favorites are the Billy Beer cans and Harley cans," Dino says. "Then there's the cans with baseball and football players. The oldest ones are the ones

Jon Mathewson, American Museum of Fly Fishing.

behind the bar. They're worth the most money. They look like the old oil cans, with the little spout."

The little spout saved brewers expensive retooling when flip-top beers appeared in the 1930s. These so-called "cone tops" lasted until 1960, when aluminum cans became popular. Today, a perfect "cone top" can fetch upwards of $600.

Dalmolin is no longer in the business of buying or trading cans for the museum, which admittedly lacks some typical museum amenities. When asked what the gift shop has to offer, Dalmolin lets out a laugh. "Museum gift shop? Bass on tap."

Reel Stories

The Vermont town of Manchester is no stranger to fly fishing. This is the home of Orvis, one of the best-known manufacturers of fly fishing equipment. Just down the street from company headquarters is the American Museum of Fly Fishing, a must-stop for any angler.

It all started simply enough back in 1968, explains museum registrar Jon Mathewson. "They were cleaning out the attic of Orvis and came across some old junk. They looked at it and figured it ought to be in a museum."

Today, the museum displays more than 1,000 rods and 400 reels.

When Chronicle's Peter Mehegan visited the museum, he took his time to closely examine a display of rods. "Now whose rods are these?" he wonders.

"That's a rod owned by Dwight Eisenhower," answers Mathewson, "used on a presidential visit to Vermont."

He moves on, "And those two?"

"This is a his-and-hers matching set, belonging to Jimmy Carter and his wife. Roslyn Carter apparently had more time to fly fish and is a more apt fly fisher, or so rumor has it."

It makes you wonder what it is about presidents and

A display at the fly fishing museum. Center and far right, the Brattleboro Museum and Art Center, Mara Wiliams.

fishing. "Grover Cleveland said he thinks there's a draw between politicians and telling tall tales—tales about fishing, or anything else," Mathewson offers.

Also on view are miniature masterpieces from the fly-tying greats of America. And when Robert Redford turned to the museum for help in researching his film, *A River Runs Through It*, he received a package of vintage reels, creels, and flies. Redford was also sent photographs of old-time anglers, just to be sure they got the hairstyles right. (For more information, phone 802–362–3300.)

A Vermont Encore

Back in the 1800s, amateur musicians were in the habit of making pilgrimages to Brattleboro, Vermont. And they haven't stopped yet.

"People came from all over the country," remarks Mara Williams, "because 'Brattleboro, Vermont' is written on the organ that their grandmother gave them, or was in their mother's house growing up. So when they stopped in Brattleboro, the first question they asked when they got off the train was always 'Where can I find out about the Estey Organ?'"

Today, they can learn about the Estey inside the old railway station, now home to the Brattleboro Museum and Art Center. What they'll find is the story of Levi Fuller, Jacob Estey, and Estey's son Julius, who developed what was to become one of Brattleboro's biggest businesses. The Estey organ was manufactured here from the 1840s through the 1950s. Rows of factory buildings employing some 700 workers produced as many as 10,000 parlor organs a year.

"I think the Estey organ is important because it's part of our cultural heritage," states museum director Williams. "Not that they're aesthetic objects, although I think that they are quite beautiful." Williams points out the workmanship, particularly the woodwork. "Even today the woodwork is a remarkable feat," she declares. "Are they great carvings in the way of a Brancusi sculpture? No, it's a different thing you're looking at."

Today, TV, DVD, and CDs are the entertainers of choice. In America's living rooms, pump organs are about as common as stereoscopes. But Brattleboro remembers. (Call 802–257–0124 to arrange your own visit.)

Birthplace of Industry

More than 200 years ago, Samuel Slater brought his formidable skills and acute business sense from England to Rhode Island. At the Slater Mill in Pawtucket, he essen-

Paul Papineau and textiles at the Slater Mill in Pawtucket, Rhode Island. Far right, Jud's Museum, all three shelves . . . .

tially gave birth to America's Industrial Revolution.

The Slater Mill is one of a breed of "living museums," which have become popular across the country. They allow us to take a step into the past and, in this particular case, learn how one mill and one man's idea changed history.

"This is the first textile mill in the United States, and it began the growth of the textile industry in the country," explains Paul Papineau, a guide at the Slater Hill Historic Site. "Cotton yard was produced here from raw cotton, using water-powered machinery for the very first time."

This museum makes its point by operating much as it did in Slater's time. An eight-ton water wheel provides power to the nearby machine shop. "We have a Butt braider, sometimes called a Maypole braider, and it's still used today to make braided rugs," Papineau points out.

The mill's first employees were children: seven boys and two girls, aged 7 through 12. Working conditions were horrendous; the children were surrounded by noise, dust, and danger. As an example, Papineau demonstrates what is called a Jacquard power loom. With a sudden thrust of the handbar, a bone-rattling shriek emerges from the loom. "You can imagine the kind of noise this would make. The people who worked it eventually became deaf."

Jud's "Cultch"

It's clear that *Yankee* magazine editor Jud Hale understands and appreciates New England's collecting culture. In fact, in his office in Dublin, New Hampshire, he's instituted his own "Witness to History" Museum, also known as "Jud's Museum." He is pleased to show off the entire collection—three overstuffed bookshelves.

"This is Jud's Museum," he begins proudly. "I've had it for 30 years in my office. I think the very first thing I got was this splinter from the Battleship Maine. People always would ask, 'How do you know it's real?' And I tell them where I got it. It had previously been owned by a library, so I could sort of know and have faith that it belonged to the Battleship Maine. That's why the motto of my museum is 'Built on Faith, Hope, and Charity.'"

The tour continues. "This is the first safety pin to fly over the North Pole. And that's a piece of fabric from the Spirit of St. Louis, Lindberg's plane, that flew over the Atlantic."

When asked about an ominous looking item on the top shelf, Jud replies that it's a real shell from Israel's 1967 war.

The question Jud hears the most is probably "What—pray tell—is the chicken?"

Jud Hale and his "Cultch" collection; not good enough to save, but too good to throw out. Below, the "brain."

"Well, this part here, is the natural history part of Jud's museum—you see, it's separated by this elastic band here." Jud indicates a barely visible band that's stretched nearly to its breaking point across the top shelf. "I just felt that any self-respecting natural history division of any museum should have something that's stuffed. So, I met a farmer who was sort of going down the tubes. And I thought, most museums would have a rhinoceros or something, but I never had seen a stuffed chicken."

Don't think Jud's Museum hasn't had its moment in the national spotlight. "You know, *USA Today* came and saw the museum. They had one word for it—'pathetic.' But I just can't throw any of this away. You could call it cultch—stuff that's not good enough to save, but too good to throw out. And a lot of museums in New England—maybe this one too—is sort of in that category."

Fortunately, perhaps, Jud's Museum is not open to the public. But he is still on the lookout for more unusual additions to his collection.

"I've been negotiating for Einstein's brain," he whispers, stepping over to a canning jar. Beneath the lid is a chunk of gray clay. "This isn't actually the brain, but this is what it'd look like if I was successful in getting it. It's out in Kansas. A Dr. Harvey has it. I saw an article in *The Wall Street Journal*. They didn't know where to put it. The Smithsonian didn't want it, so I wrote a nice letter saying I'd put it in Jud's Museum." According to Jud, there was one hitch: "The Einstein family didn't want it on public display. So I've written back saying I wouldn't put it on public display. I promise—if I do get Einstein's brain, I'll keep it in my desk drawer."

U P D A T E : Jud Hale has made a few new additions to his museum, including an autographed photo of Ted Williams and Dom DiMaggio. As for the stuffed chicken, it may need a talent agent soon. Not only was it seen on Chronicle, Jud brought it with him for an appearance on NBC's *Today* show, where he attempted to convince Katie Couric that the chicken was only hypnotized, not dead. But you have to wake up pretty early in the morning to get one over on Katie Couric—she was not persuaded.

The MILL RIVER DISASTER

May 16, 1874, brought an epic tragedy to Massachusetts' Berkshire Hills. Over a billion gallons of water destroyed four towns and took the lives of 144 people. Filled with both horror and heroism, the tale of the Mill River flood is all but forgotten. In the spring of 1993, Chronicle brought the story to television for the very first time.

In the mid-1800s, the Mill River in western Massachusetts provided water power to mills and factories in the small towns just above Northampton, bringing life to villages such as Williamsburg and Haydenville. The river spun the water wheels and generated power for a number of small industrial enterprises including a button factory, a brass works, and a woolen mill. Inside the factories, Irish and Canadian immigrants toiled long hours for about a dollar a day. But in summer, the waters of the Mill River slowed to a trickle and the factories had to close. Mill owners decided to build a reservoir upstream, collecting water in the spring that could be released during the dry months to keep the wheels of commerce spinning all summer long.

Collins Graves

Heavy rains in the spring of 1874 filled the reservoir to capacity; there was plenty of water to keep the factories humming. But on the morning of May 16, George Cheney, gatekeeper at the dam, noticed a serious breach at the dam's base. He knew it was only a matter of time before the dam would burst and a billion gallons of water would go thundering toward the communities below. Cheney jumped on a horse and raced toward Williamsburg, three miles downstream. He went straight to the home of O.G. Spellman, overseer of the dam. At first Spellman didn't believe Cheney, and said the dam could never fail. Crucial time was lost before Cheney convinced Spellman that a catastrophe was about to occur.

While Cheney was racing to Williamsburg, a farmer named Robert Loud looked across the valley and saw that large cracks were developing in the dam. Having no horse, Loud started running to warn the people of Williamsburg. He raced to the Adams Flouring Mill. Out of breath, he threw a stick at the window and pointed upstream, giving workers a few precious seconds to escape.

Farmer Collins Graves was in his horse-drawn wagon delivering milk in Williamsburg. He heard George

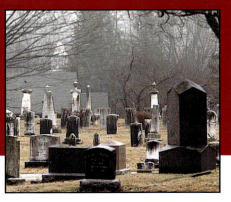

George Cheney, at right.

Cheney's frantic tale and raced south in his carriage to warn people downstream. Running just a few minutes ahead of the flood, Graves entered Skinnerville and warned workers in the silk mill. Most of them escaped in time. Though the raging water obliterated the mill and carried houses away like bobbing corks, Graves's warning saved many lives.

The wave of destruction reached 20 feet high—an angry torrent of shattered wood, jagged metal, rocks, farm equipment, wagons, and fences, as well as human and animal corpses. After ripping through four communities, the flood finally inundated a meadow in Florence. The water and debris spread out across the meadow and the tremendous energy behind the flood was finally spent.

It all took less than an hour. One hundred forty-four people lost their lives; a thousand were made homeless. The task of looking for victims was a grim one. The bodies of three children could not be identified; one man was

never found. An inquest revealed that the dam had not been built to specifications. But no one was ever prosecuted and no lawsuits were ever filed.

Today, there is little evidence of the flood. A small plaque in Haydenville is the only public monument to the men, women, and children who lost their lives. In the hills above the river valley, weathered gravestones mark the human tragedy of the Mill River disaster.

OUT THERE

They are out there—hidden in the hills, holed up in the hollows. The Northeast's nooks and crannies provide the perfect soil for cultivating a stubborn individuality and a peculiar originality. In 1999 Chronicle's Mary Richardson combed the region in search of New England nonconformists.

The Gaugin of Garbage

He wears a plaid jacket of red and black—the sort worn by most everyone here in Harmony, Maine. But the jacket is the one and only thing that's commonplace about Wally Warren. From his cap hangs a fringe of small pink pom-poms. At the entrance to his property is a colorful, fanciful collage made entirely of recycled materials. "Welcome to the Wall of Refuse," he exclaims with a flourish of pride. This is garbage all right—garbage that's found its way to art galleries from Maine to Montana.

Wally Warren and his Wall of Refuse.

For thirty years, Warren has been collecting, painting, and putting up trash. He sees one of his walls as a contribution to his neighbors. "I don't know if the community realizes it or not," he says, "but this is for them."

Parts from dishwashers and washing machines. Hubcaps and windshield wipers. Frying pans. Computer keyboards. Warren is inspired by it all. He describes himself as a "post-apocalyptic artist," dwelling in what might be called the last stop in the technological food chain. His current project is a perfect example. "For the last several years I've been building these model cities out of broken-down computer parts and TV parts," he says. Pointing to one unrecognizable piece of plastic, he explains, "This came out of a TV. In fact, this was a TV that worked until a few weeks ago! Until I broke it!"

Warren points out that his work has a biological bent. "I'm a microbe. I'm breaking stuff down, digesting stuff," he declares. "I break things down all the time—not just computers and TV sets, but vacuum cleaners, cars—especially cars. I just want to break them down, and chew them up! Spit them out and rebuild them into something that's different and beautiful."

Fume Hall of Famer Brian Patton (left) and odor-ologist Buddy Lapidus (right).

Warren's craving for color may be the result of too many long gray winters in the Maine woods. "New England, you know it's such a drab place! People think everything has to be green," he laments. "What's wrong with a little red or yellow? What's wrong with a little magenta?"

Warren's junk art can be found in private collections all over the country. His cabin is crammed with pieces in progress. For those who seem befuddled, he gladly provides translations for his work. "These plugs are saying 'Ooh, Ooh, Great One!'" he says. "I have a candle that goes in the middle and it's like the plugs are worshiping the candle, saying 'This is where it came from—this is the light!'"

It's a somewhat solitary life Warren leads, but it gives him the space he needs to get where he wants to go. "This is a way of affirming myself and my existence in a barren landscape," he muses. "This isn't just a matter of nuts and bolts and chainsaws and trucks. It's a matter of form—a matter of beauty."

Among his new projects is a model city "made of computer detritus." It was commissioned by the State of Maine and will become a permanent installation in the new Statehouse.

Warren emphasizes that visitors are welcome to tour his outdoor sculpture site. "If you're on Route 154, it's unavoidable anyway," he says, "so just stop in."

Follow Your Nose

Ah, springtime in New England. The smell of earth awakening after a long frozen slumber. The intoxicating perfume of blooming flowers. And the rich, gamy aroma of rotten sneakers. Bring on the rotten and oh-so-smelly footwear. In Montpelier, Vermont, the annual Odor-Eaters Rotten Sneaker Contest is under way.

"Excellent hole there," a judge comments to one contestant. "And you've gone the extra mile by not washing your feet for a while—haven't you? Good for you!"

Now in its twenty-fourth year, the contest features celebrity odor-ologist Buddy Lapidus. Call him the Einstein of Odor. He is the man who suffered for us all—sacrificing his nostrils to invent Odor-Eaters. "I often tell people it was a roommate of mine who had smelly feet. Actually, it was my wife," Lapidus confesses. "I don't like to talk about that too much."

We catch up with two-time contest winner Brian Patton. "I was six years old when I won the first time, and fifteen when I won last year," Brian exclaims proudly. Now retired, Patton is a giant in the world of malodor. He

Teenie, Bob, some toys, and Boss Hog. Visitors claim a trip to Teenie's just wouldn't be complete without seeing the Boss.

is the only person to produce a stench powerful enough to have two pairs of shoes enshrined in the Hall of Fumes.

"Yeah," he beams. "These are mine from last year, and these are mine from back in '89. Most people say it's not something to be proud of, but I am."

No kidding—people travel to Montpelier's Rec Center from as far away as Alaska and Italy to take part in this contest. This time, Brian Patton passes his baton to number 110: Chelsea Hours, who is returning home to West Virginia in triumph—the Stinkiest Sneaker Award cradled in her arms.

Fine Feathered Farm

It's an age-old question: which came first—the chicken or the museum? At Teenie's Tiny Poultry Farm and Museum outside Rutland, Vermont, it doesn't really matter, because the price is right.

"No charge to get in—it's all free!" exclaims the owner. "We love to have people come. No set hours. If we're home, we'll gladly take them over." Teenie's Tiny Poultry Farm is located on Teenie's Tiny Road. Both are named after—you guessed it—Teenie. "That's me," says Christine Bearor. "I had an aunt whose name was also Christine. She had a nickname, Nini. So she gave me the

nickname of Teenie. It's been Teenie ever since."

This is one of the oddest museums you'll ever come across. What is in its collection? Chainsaws, toys, farm equipment, live animals . . . frankly, it's easier to list what *isn't* here than to inventory all that's tucked into the corners of Teenie's various outbuildings.

The tour begins with Teenie's flocks of exotic birds. Admiring a stately peacock, she reflects, "The male is always prettier than the female—only in the bird species." There are other curious creatures, beginning with the deer who favors chewing on cigarettes. "It's good for him," Teenie explains. "Keeps the worms out of him. He gets one a day."

As for the rest of the collection, Teenie's husband, Bob, is to blame for most of it. "We started with the farm machinery and the gas engines and things, and it just kept ballooning. We just kept buying," Bob says. "We've got barnfuls now! We're adding on to the museum and still, we don't know where to put it all. But," he adds sheepishly, "we're still buying!"

You name it: train sets, gas pumps, milk separators, matchbox cars—even a gold-plated motorcycle. Bob says one visitor made him an offer of $100,000 for the bike, but he turned it down. The oddest of all in this odd collection

The Orgone Energy Observatory, the cloud buster rain making device, and museum guide Kathy Steward.

is an assortment of slightly used jail cells.

Presiding over the sprawling compound is the one and only Boss Hog, an English bulldog. "A lot of visitors come and, if Boss Hog isn't out, they'll make a special request to see him," Bob says. "A visit to Teenie's just wouldn't be complete without seeing the Boss."

Mainely Science?

Overlooking Rangeley Lake in western Maine is Orgonon, home of the late psychoanalyst and scientist, Wilhelm Reich. It is a massive, multiroomed structure built of stone. Today, the public is welcome inside the Orgone Energy Observatory to view Reich's intriguing inventions, the equipment used in his experiments, and his artwork.

Museum guide Kathy Steward grew up in Rangeley and went to school with Reich's son. She says townspeople weren't sure what to make of the immigrant family. "In a small town you get lots of rumors," Steward says. "Anything they can't see or understand or put their finger on, then there's always talk."

And Reich gave them plenty to talk about. For one

Wilhem Reich
Courtesy: Orgonon

thing, he built fierce-looking rainmaking devices called cloud busters. "When they first starting hauling one of the cloud busters around in the back of a truck," recalls Steward, "there were some who would say it was some new kind of machine gun. And then there were others who'd say, 'Oh, it looks like a new milking machine!'"

A onetime associate of Sigmund Freud, Reich was intrigued by energy functions in human emotions. The major project of his career was his attempt to prove the existence of what he dubbed orgone—a ubiquitous, invisible energy source. That search led to his best-known invention. "It's called the Orgone Energy Accumulator," Steward explains, "and it was used to concentrate energy from the atmosphere in a small area."

Reich believed his accumulator could recharge a person's energies. Smaller devices would zero in on specific physical problems. "There are many people who still use accumulators, students of Reich who kept one, and people who built their own." Steward says. "I've tried it myself and gotten good results—I can feel it."

Though she doesn't think of herself as a disciple of

A different view of the cloud buster, and the sunset over Rangeley Lake—an inspiration? At right, the accumulator.

the good doctor, Steward keeps an open mind. "I just don't know. You ask yourself, 'Would this have healed without the accumulator?' Or, 'Would someone who didn't use it get the same results?' You just don't know."

Unlike Steward, the U.S. government had no interest in keeping an open mind; in 1956, Reich was thrown in jail on a contempt of court conviction stemming from fraud charges brought by the Food and Drug Administration. "They felt there was no such thing as orgone energy. So therefore he was a quack," she says.

Reich died in prison the following year. Even so, his ideas about orgone energy, though hard to grasp, are still floating around out there.

The Wilhelm Reich Museum is open to the public during the summer and by appointment. For more information, see www.somtel.com/~wreich/ or call 207–864–3443.

UPDATE: As technology advances, so does Warren. His newest medium is the satellite dish. He's collected and painted several discarded dishes, and scattered them across his five acres. "It looks like a yardful of mushrooms," he reports.

Among the judges for the annual Odor Eaters contest is NASA's "master sniffer." George Aldrich performs odor panel tests for astronauts to prevent toxic odors from entering the confined crew environment. Put simply, Aldrich's job is to ensure that foul-smelling odors don't make the astronauts sick while they're in space.

As you might guess, Bob and Teenie are still at it. They've converted two old bunkhouses into additional museums for their collections. One will house Teenie's handmade artificial snowmen. And the other? "Oh, some antique gas pumps, I guess," Bob says, "and more milk separators. Whatever. I just keep adding." What's more, they've added a trout pond out back, complete with an observation deck. And they're working on rebuilding a '71 Chevy Impala convertible, from the ground up. The Bearors recommend that visitors call ahead before driving up. (For more information, call 802–773–2637.)

A Harvest *to* Remember

When the days grow short and the leaves fall and flame, it is harvest time in New England. With a ripe, full moon hanging in the sky, Chronicle set off to capture the colors and traditions of the season. Our 1995 trip took us from the cranberry bogs of Cape Cod to Vermont's apple orchards to the far reaches of Maine's potato fields.

A Berry Good Crop

On a sunny morning in southeastern Massachusetts, a deep shade of red is framed by a crisp blue sky. The bold colors can mean only one thing: it's time to bring in the cranberry crop.

Betty Brown and her crew are harvesting bogs in Carver. "These bogs were started by my grandfather. In the 1930s, he planted the main part of the acreage, and then my father and uncle worked it all through the '50s," Betty explains. "When I was a kid, I thought this was absolutely the perfect way to make a living. What I really hated was that school started at the same time as harvest, and just when I was really getting into it, they would make me go to school. I thought that was a terrible cheat."

When Betty was growing up, farming was not a career choice for women. So she went off to college, earned a Ph.D. in American Literature, and built a career as an academic librarian. But when her father decided to retire and sell the land, Betty traded her career for a chance to run the family farm. She has not looked back.

"When you think of some bogs, like in Wisconsin, they're perfect rectangles. But this is New England, so everything is tucked into little necks and hollows," Betty says. "Our bogs conform to the shape of the land, so in

Harvesting the cranberries.

Pumpkin Bowling—a favored activity at the World Pumpkin Games Federation, Ashfield, Massachusetts.

some senses it's not very easy for us to harvest. Sometimes it takes a while. We use paddles and sweep all the berries off. My father has a rule. He says, 'You don't have to be too fussy; you just have to get every berry.'"

Owning a cranberry bog is not without worries, but for Betty, the payoff is priceless. "I alternate between being really worried about the crop and really focusing on what I'm doing," she admits. "And then every once in a while I'll be standing in the water and it'll be a perfect day, and you'll be warm and comfortable, the sun will be shining, there will be foliage all around you, and there's these gorgeous red berries and you just know it can't *get* any better than this."

If only those moments could last. "Then there's the other days," Betty laughs, "when it's about 45 degrees, there's a 35-mile-per-hour wind, and it's raining. You're wet from knees down because your waders are leaking, and you've got rain running down your neck."

Pumpkin Games

They make good pies and terrific jack-o'-lanterns. Fairy tales tell us that, in an emergency, they'll make a passable horse-drawn carriage. And, according to residents of Ashfield, Massachusetts, pumpkins are also superior sporting goods.

As proof, Ashfield offers the World Pumpkin Games, a fun-filled, tongue-in-cheek event hosted by the town's "World Pumpkin Games Federation." Rain or shine, the town comes out for this annual frolic. Federation "Commissioner" Dick Evans ticks off the events: "There's the circular pumpkin pass, pumpkin relay matches, the add-a-pumpkin team relay, pumpkin field hockey," he begins. Get the concept?

"Pumpkin bowling—now that's a good one," Dick continues. "But if you want to get close and watch, be sure you're not in the line of a bowling ball!" And what about bowling pins? A set of ten zucchini works just fine.

"If there's a tie at the end of the competition, then we have a sudden pumpkin death," Evans explains. Has there even been a playoff? Dick doesn't have the faintest idea. "In our own way, we're fastidious about records," he replies. "There has never been a single record of a single game ever recorded."

Tater Talk

Maine's Aroostook County is as far north as you can go in New England. As one farmer puts it, "It's not quite the end of the earth, but you can see the end from here."

Emily Hart working the potato harvest, Aroostook County, Maine.

This is potato country: rolling terrain with a soil rich in calcium and limestone. The growing season is short: only 120 days from the last frost of spring to the first frost of fall. When potatoes reach their full size, the harvest is a race against nature.

Since the 1960s, farmers in Aroostook County have relied upon a popular TV show to keep them informed during harvest season. It's the "Potato Pickers Special," hosted by Dave Lavway. The show is a combination weather report, bulletin board, and informal talk show; and it may well be the only show in the country where guests are regularly served breakfast, right on the air.

"We run at 4:30 to 6:30 every morning, Monday through Saturday, during harvest season," Lavway explains. "Basically, we read messages to crews as to when they're going to start. We'll also read help-wanted messages—if somebody's looking for a job, or some grower's looking for help that day, we'll do that too."

Aroostook County grows 90 percent of Maine's annual potato crop, about 70,000 acres worth. Few potatoes are picked by hand these days; mechanical harvesters do most of the work. But traditions die hard, and most of the county's public schools are still let out for three weeks so that students can earn a bit of extra cash, helping to haul in the crops. Some schools have ended the practice, claiming that more kids visit the malls than the fields. But not Emily Hart. A junior at Central High, she's worked the harvest on her uncle's farm for the past five years. "I get up about 5:00 in the morning," Emily says. "I go to whatever field they tell me to go to, and then I wait 'til my uncle hollers, 'C'mon girls!'"

"We have a very special bond here with the land, I believe," adds Lavway. "When we were young, our mothers would get us out of bed at 4:00 or 4:30, and boy, it was tough to roll out of bed as a teenager to go and pick potatoes. But you learned the meaning of hard work."

You also learn about what it's like when a community shares a common cause. "When harvest season rolls around, everybody is tuned into it, everybody's talking about it," Lavway says. "You go into the coffee shops, everybody's talking about what the potatoes look like: 'How's the quality?' 'What's the yield?' The whole society up here focuses on the harvest and getting it in."

Core Values

The professional crews and the pick-your-own crowd are out in force at Dwight Miller's apple farm in Dummerston, Vermont. At harvest time, it's "all hands on deck"

Dwight Miller overseeing the apple harvest.

here. In addition to the 30 itinerant pickers from Mexico and Florida, Miller's daughters, sons, and in-laws are enlisted to help with the picking, packing, shipping, and retail operations. "There's never a day that there's not something going on here," Dwight says. "It takes a lot of patience, a lot of knowledge of what you're doing."

And for Dwight, it also seems like the thing that it takes a lot of now is *money.* He feels the pressure. "The bills seem to roll in faster, sometimes, than the money does," he sighs. "Farmers don't mind working hard hours; we don't mind working in the cold, and the heat, and the rain, as long as we can pay our bills and make a decent living."

The business of farming has grown more complex and competitive since the Miller family started these orchards four generations ago. Dwight's son, Reid, runs the daily operation now. He keeps it going by tapping diverse markets. "The production of any farm product, in the harvesting, marketing, and packaging, is very difficult," Reid contends. "Of course, when you go into a supermarket, and it's sitting there—whether it's the container of milk or the bag of apples—it's pretty simple. But to actually go from the soil and the water and the sunshine to get to that point—boy, is it a lot of work! You really have to have nerves of steel to stay at it all the time and make it work."

And when it comes to apples trees, adds Dwight, beauty is definitely in the eye of the beholder. He realizes that the average person sees a tree that's loaded with apples and says 'Isn't that beautiful!' Not him, though. "When that tree is *picked*, and there's not one apple left, that's when I say, 'Boy, is that beautiful!'"

Just Desserts

What would a New England harvest be without dessert? In Dummerston they've got a dazzling display of desserts, cooked up every year around this time. But the ladies of Dummerston can't start up their stoves until the key ingredient is picked from the trees.

Dwight Miller's apples are at the core of the 1,500 pies baked in just two weeks for the Dummerston Congregational Church's annual fundraiser. Bess Richardson, co-chair of the Pie Festival, describes the process. "We start around 8:00 A.M., slicing apples, peeling them, coring them. This group of people over here," she says, indicating the slicing committee, "you don't want to argue with them. They're the ones with the knives."

Young, old, experienced, and not-so-experienced—everyone comes out to help in this 30-year-old tradition. "It's not just a church affair, it's a community affair,"

Prepping for the Dummerston Pie Festival.

Richardson says. "It's lively. We tell jokes, share stories. I guess it's a lot like a quilting bee."

Inside the sanctuary on Sale Sunday, it's time to replace parishioners with pies. It's not an easy job. "We take the pew cushions off and we fill the pews with pies," Richardson explains. "Then we fill the floor with pies. Pies everywhere. Then at 10:30, the church bell rings, so people know it's time to buy the pies."

UPDATE: Ashfield's Pumpkin Games are "going stronger than ever," reports Game Commissioner Dick Evans. Part of the town's annual fall festival, they begin "precisely at noon" on the Saturday preceding Columbus Day. Newer events include "pumpkin posture," which requires participants to walk while balancing pumpkins atop their heads—no hands, please! Another new entry is pumpkin hockey. Those zucchini bowling pins are recycled as hockey sticks.

The Dummerston Pie Festival is held every year on the Sunday preceding Columbus Day. It begins at 10:30 A.M. and runs until the last piece of pie is sold. The event has developed quite a following—including a group of Harley Davidson enthusiasts who ride up from Massachusetts every year. In 2000, more than 200 motorcycles graced the town for Sale Sunday. According to Bess Richardson, "You can hear them coming from miles away."

And the puck? You guessed it: a pumpkin.

"Potato Pickers Special" is still a staple on WAGM-TV in Maine. But one feature has disappeared: breakfast is no longer on the program's menu. This wasn't a cost-cutting decision, explains Creative Services Director Jason York. "We had a little grease fire one morning, and we came to realize that breakfast created a fire hazard."

You can still "pick your own" at Dwight Miller's orchard, but now you'll be plucking organic apples off the trees. The Millers switched from conventional growing to become one of the largest certified organic orchards in the East. "It's trial and error," Reid's wife, Malah, reports. "We're learning as we go." Miller apples continue to play a starring role in the Congregational Church Pie Festival. "After all," Malah points out, "not only are we members of the church . . . my mother-in-law is the festival co-chair!"

ALL-AMERICAN THREE-DECKERS

Three floors, and so many stories. Plain or fancy, run-down or renovated, the three-decker house is uniquely New England. In the fall of 2000, Chronicle's Peter Mehegan went in search of the three-decker's origin. Along the way, he discovered some remarkable stories, and revisited the home where he grew up.

Like the Bunker Hill Monument and the Old North Church, the three-decker house is part of the Boston landscape. While New Englanders take these ubiquitous houses for granted, they are all but nonexistent in other parts of the country.

Three-deckers were the answer to Boston's housing shortage at the turn of the 19th century. As immigrants flooded the city, the houses went up at a furious pace—roughly 16,000 between 1890 and 1930. The three-decker offered an affordable and sometimes profitable formula to first-time homebuyers.

"You could rent out the top two floors and live almost rent-free," explains Howard Husock, who conducted a study of three-deckers at Harvard University's Kennedy School of Government. "You could rent to your father-in-law, your mother-in-law, or whoever—and deal with family problems that way!"

The definition of a three-decker? A freestanding, wood frame structure with three equal living spaces occupying its own narrow lot. The three-decker was a step up from the old row house tenements, permitting a welcome dose of sunlight and providing a bit of green space.

"Smaller builders were the ones who put up the three-deckers," Husock says. "And they all put their own stamp of originality on them. There's the so-called cracker box three-decker—very common—with the three porches and no adornments. But you've also got very elaborate three-deckers, with craftsmen and tradesmen adding their own marks."

Ed Forry, born and bred in Dorchester and the publisher of *The Dorchester Reporter*, says three-deckers help differentiate the city's natives from newcomers: "You can tell who's arrived in this town since 1980 or so. If they call them *triple* deckers, they didn't grow up here. But if they're like you and me," he says to Dorchester-born Peter, "well, we call them *three*-deckers."

A Must-Have for Hollywood

Joe Keating's three-decker home at 259 E Street in South Boston has been in the family since the early 1940s, when his wife's grandmother bought it. "All of my children have lived here. My wife's brothers and sisters have lived here. My mother and my sister have lived here. Now, it's my nieces who are living on the first floor."

Three-decker fans Joe Keating (left) and Ed Forry (right).

Number 259 E Street was just another Southie three-decker until one day, "my mother and sister were living downstairs and someone knocked on the door." That "someone" was from Hollywood, the director of an upcoming movie titled *Good Will Hunting*, starring Matt Damon, Ben Affleck, and Robin Williams.

"He said that one of the art directors or the set directors or somebody saw the color of the house, and said he just had to have this house in the movie," Keating recalls. "Maybe you remember the scene: at the end of the movie they used the front of the house, when Matt Damon came up and put the letter in the mailbox and you could see Robin Williams through the second floor window."

All Roads Lead to Worcester

Searching for the origins of the three-decker, the road leads to Worcester, Massachusetts, where a colorful variety of three-deckers dominates the cityscape. Although no one knows for certain if these houses are a Worcester invention, Douglas Johnson of Worcester's Clark University says that the city does take credit as the first to call them "three-deckers."

Johnson, a professor of cultural geography, is fascinated by the buildings. "They are part of our heritage, and they're interesting as a kind of 'folk housing.'" Johnson

took Peter on a tour of Worcester's three-decker neighborhoods. He knows these streets well, having conducted an extensive survey of Worcester's shrinking bounty. "At one time, the city may have had over 5,000 three-deckers," Johnson explains. "When we did the survey, there were just over 4,000. Today, there are considerably fewer." One hundred fifty of those left have been placed on the National Historic Register.

Johnson says the collection of buildings in the Vernon Hill neighborhood on Perry Street may well represent the finest group of four or five late-Colonial revival buildings in Worcester. The roofs, columns, and ornaments are of all shapes and sizes. And there are curiosities called laundry porches where, as he explains, "the reel can be cranked into the porch, and the clothes hung up on it, and then cranked outside."

Johnson calls Worcester's three-deckers an "ordinary landscape," too familiar or too young to be treasured. But take note now, he warns, before it's too late. With each house that falls victim to fire or redevelopment, a piece of the past is erased forever.

Monument

Neptune Road in East Boston was once lined with three-deckers. "There were forty or forty-five homes here,"

Artist Loring Coleman and Number 18.

remembers former resident Leo Gleason. "We were Italian, Irish, some Portuguese families." When asked whether they were all big families, Gleason told Peter: "Big!?! We had our own athletic team—the Neptunes!"

Today, Gleason's boyhood home is a vacant lot. It is hard to envision 21 families living here. In the 1960s, "progress" came to Neptune Road in the form of bulldozers. The street happened to stand in the path of the Massachusetts Port Authority's plan to extend a runway at Logan Airport. And so a neighborhood of three-deckers was decimated, along with 40 seaside acres of nearby Wood Island Park, designed by Frederick Law Olmsted.

Some of the Neptune Road houses were moved; most were torn down. The only one surviving is Number 18.

It was on a trip home from Logan Airport that artist Loring Coleman noticed 18 Neptune Road. "I saw this image, like a monolith, standing in a field of grass," Coleman says. "It was so lonely. You don't usually see three-deckers by themselves. Generally, they are part of a community. I couldn't get the feeling out of my mind that there had been a lot going on in there."

To Coleman's eyes, the house was a visual delight. "The little teeth carvings under the windows. The little

squares. Marvelous," he remembers. "And the frieze around the top was like a crown—almost like a birthday cake, all this detail." He wanted to put the house on canvas.

For Coleman, the one missing element was the house's history. Why did it stand alone? Coleman's answer came from an odd source. "I got very ill at Christmas time," he recalls. "I was at Emerson Hospital in Concord when my surgeon, Dr. Seymour DiMare, came in." When DiMare asked what Coleman was working on, "I told him about the Neptune Road painting and he said 'Oh my God, I was born right near there!'"

Thanks to this remarkable coincidence, the house's story would at last be complete for Coleman. In exchange, Coleman had opened a floodgate of memories for Dr. DiMare. "Those houses were people's homes—immigrants' homes," DiMare says. "Those homes were what symbolized their hope in this new world. Loring sensed some of that emotion in the house, and he faithfully reproduced all of the deterioration of the house—yet all of its beauty too."

Coleman titled his painting *Monument*, a title Dr. DiMare says works perfectly. "It's a fitting monument to the dreams that were extinguished by having removed all

Dr. Seymour DiMare reminiscing on the romance of the three-decker.

those homes," he reflects. Coleman adds, "I thought this was a monument to the people who withstood the pressure to leave their neighborhood. They are anonymous people to me, but they are important people to me."

You Can Take the Boy Out of Dorchester

This assignment gave Chronicle's Peter Mehegan the perfect excuse to do something he's wanted to do for some time: return to his boyhood home. He stood outside the house and spoke directly to the camera. "This three-decker on Fuller Street in Dorchester was home to the Mehegans for part of my childhood. My grandmother and her sister lived on the first floor, we lived on the second, and my father's cousins lived on the third. It was comfortable, inexpensive housing for the times. And, it was home."

Residents of the house watched from their window as Peter and the Chronicle crew finished their videotaping. Eventually, one woman stepped outside. "May I help you?" she asked Peter. "I used to live here," he began, and then went on to explain his assignment. The woman seemed satisfied and went back indoors. It looked as

> The Heritage Harbor Museum in Providence, Rhode Island, scheduled to open in 2003, will feature a full-scale three-decker house. For more information, see the museum's Web site: www.heritageharbor.org.

though the invitation Peter had hoped for would not be forthcoming. Then, the door opened a second time. Peter was invited inside, *without* our Chronicle cameras.

With one glimpse of the old apartment, Peter's own three-decker memories were revived. "It wasn't the life of *one* family—it was open house for *three* families. It was like lifestyles of the rich and famous—Dorchester style," Peter recalls. "Three places to live, to visit, to eat—all under one roof. I especially remember when my cousins upstairs got the first television set in the neighborhood—one of those black and white sets, with the magnifying glasses over the screen. You needed the magnifying glass because the screen was so small."

How far television has come since those days—and how far Peter's come along with it.

UPDATE: Number 18 Neptune Road was recently purchased by Americo Venti, who has lived on the street since 1926. He's been a tenant at 18 Neptune for years, and bought it when the former owner passed away. As a housewarming gift, Loring Coleman generously presented Venti with a framed copy of *Monument*.

FILLING
in the GAPS

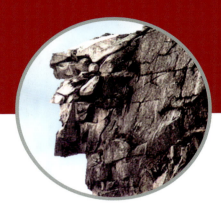

They are openings in the high mountain country. Known as gaps or passes in other parts of the U.S., they're called notches in New England. No other state is more marked by its notches than New Hampshire, as Chronicle's Mary Richardson discovered in the fall of 1994.

Most of the Granite State's notches sit on government-owned parkland. But there is one exception: Crawford Notch, home to the state's smallest town, Hart's Location.

The population of Hart's Location hovers around 40 people, give or take a few. Marion Varney and her husband are the oldest residents, and the busiest. When winter nears, it's time to pull out the chain saws and start cutting wood.

The Town Hall for Hart's Location is located in Marion's basement, next to the washer and dryer, over by the fruit preserves. But you can't find much else in the way of municipality. Hart's Location has no police department, no fire department, no mayor, no school, no post office, and no church. What it does have is long, hard winters, and a nice view of the Mount Washington Hotel.

Train Spotting

How do you get through a notch? Trains were the traditional way in Crawford Notch. And now they are again, in foliage season. Lines that long lay abandoned are being reborn to take tourists leaf peeping. The Conway Scenic Railroad re-opened tracks last used in the 1980s in order to run excursion trains up the notch.

Pinkham Notch is flanked by two mountains and overshadowed by one of them—Mount Washington—the highest peak in the Northeast. There are no permanent residents in Pinkham Notch, but plenty of temporary ones, who take part in the school programs at the Appalachian Mountain Club's camp.

What they study is weather—very bad weather. Folks around here say Mount Washington has the worst

Seeing the forest and *the trees . . .*
The view along the Conway Scenic
Railroad, above, and Marion Varney,
right.

The Town Hall, Hart's Location,
New Hampshire.

weather in the world. For proof, take a ride up the seven-mile Mount Washington Auto Road. En route, you leave a warm, sunny autumn day and enter a sub-freezing alpine wasteland. It's the equivalent of taking a 700-mile trip to the northern reaches of Canada, in just 20 minutes.

Rime ice appears by the side of the road, facing sideways into the wind like feathery, horizontal icicles.

At the summit, the swiftness of the weather changes on Mount Washington is illustrated in vivid detail. A van sits entombed in ice and snow. The owner has to hope for a late autumn thaw—or investigate alternative transportation.

The Old Man

Franconia Notch is the most heavily traveled notch in New England, and probably the most recognizable. That's because it's got a famous face: the Old Man of the Mountain. (see inset photo opposite page.)

European settlers discovered the Man in 1805. Trains, tourists, and grand hotels soon followed, as the White Mountains became a national attraction. But in the twentieth century, tourist patterns changed, and one by one, the hotels closed or burned down. Today, as the Old Man peers down from his perch, he looks over mountains that may be the wildest they have been in a century.

UPDATE: The population of Hart's Location is now 36 people. Marion Varney, who makes it a point to ski every day in season, continues to be the town's busiest citizen. In 1997, she self published a book about her community: *Hart's Location in Crawford Notch: New Hampshire's Smallest Town.*

Looking for more information on the notches? Phone the Pinkham Notch Visitor Center, 603–466–2721, or log on to the White Mountains Info Server at www.cs.dartmouth.edu/whites/index.html.

NEW ENGLAND'S STRANGEST STORIES

In New England, storytelling is more than a way to pass the time. It helps define us and preserve our heritage. Until now, some of our strangest stories were known by just a handful of New Englanders. Others were hidden in old pamphlets and long-ignored books. But Chronicle is committed to changing all that. Here's a sampling from 1995 that deserves another telling . . . and another . . . and another.

The Petrified Indian Boy

Just above Turners Falls, Massachusetts, back in 1871, two young boys made an amazing discovery. They had been rabbit hunting in the company of a Mr. George Parsons of Springfield, when something along the clay banks of the Connecticut River drew their dog's attention. They soon uncovered what appeared to be human remains.

It looked to be a boy, perhaps an Indian boy. The threesome brought their find to the Mansion House Hotel in Greenfield. When word got out, crowds gathered at the hotel and demanded to see the body. It didn't take long for George Parsons to figure out that he should charge admission—a dime a head. That very first day, he collected the sum of $160 from "Lo, The Poor Petrified Indian Boy."

Soon, the petrified boy drew national attention, and

"Lo, The Poor Petrified Indian Boy."

received a stamp of authenticity from no less than Governor John Stewart of Vermont, who proclaimed that these were truly the fossilized remains of an Indian boy. "Lo" became one of New England's favorite travelling road shows, until he was purchased and put on display at 104 Washington Street in Boston. Here, police made a discovery of their own. The boy was a fake, the owner was fined, and the exhibit shut down.

Once the hoax was public, "Lo" disappeared. It wasn't until 1994 that he turned up again—in a museum owned by Henry Sheldon in Middlebury, Vermont. But don't look for Lo on exhibit. As Chronicle's Peter Mehegan discovered, he's been hidden in the museum's basement for nearly a century.

Peter and museum director Julie Bressor make their way down the stairs and over to a coffin-like box. "Holy

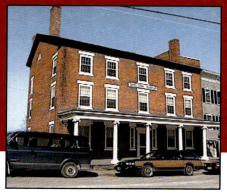

Courtesy: The Sheldon Museum

The Sheldon Museum and founder Henry Sheldon. At far right, John Graye's last message, or 19th-century humbug?

smoke! Look at that! That's the way it was found?" The two stand over the figure, resting inside the fabric-lined box.

"That's the way we've always had it here," Bressor answers. "It came to the museum in 1894, and it's been here ever since."

"Is it clearly a hoax?"

"Absolutely. I think it's here because it amused the museum's founder." Bressor goes on to explain why Lo is no longer on display. "It had been upstairs in the museum's card room, where founder Henry Sheldon put it. But when we started offering tours for schoolchildren, there seemed to be a lot of trepidation when it came time to go into the card room, so it finally became relegated to the basement."

We wanted to know more about Henry Sheldon, a man whose tastes clearly ran to the unusual.

"He loved oddities, things that were different," Bressor answers. "And he had a wonderful eye for things. He collected furniture, paintings, tools—anything that related to the history of Middlebury."

But Sheldon's legacy isn't restricted to Americana. He is the force behind an exceptional headstone in Middle-bury's Old West Cemetery bearing the date, "1883 B.C."

It turns out that Sheldon had been storing an Egyptian mummy in his attic. It wasn't discovered until 1945, long after Sheldon's death, after exposure to the Vermont weather had caused the mummy to decompose. So local authorities cremated the remains and, to this day, you can still find the ashes of Egyptian Prince "Amun Her Kepeshef, Aged 2 Years, Son of Sen Woset, King of Egypt, Died 1883 B.C." right in the middle of Middlebury.

Last Words

On riverbanks near Vermont's Lake Champlain, another mystery unfolds. Back in 1853, two marble workers were digging sand along the Missisquoi River in Swanton. They uncovered a small lead tube plugged with pine pitch. When they opened the tube, they found a message written in old English. "This is the solme [sic] day I must now die. This is the 90th day since we left the ship. All are perished, and on the banks of this river, I die." The note is signed "John Graye, November 29, 1564."

If the date is real, then John Graye died on this spot 45 years before Samuel de Champlain became the first

President Roosevelt's 1902 close call.

known white man to discover the lake.

But is the message genuine? Or is it another 19th-century humbug? We'll never know. The original lead tube and paper have been missing for years. Only a copy remains, leaving us to wonder whether a lone stranded sailor froze to death near the shores of Lake Champlain some 400 years ago.

A President in Peril

It's a piece of film that's both rare and seldom shown. Recorded on August 26, 1902, it shows President Theodore Roosevelt addressing a crowd in Lynn, Massachusetts. Not only is it the only surviving film of Roosevelt in New England—it was nearly the last film ever taken of him.

One week later, a bizarre accident occurred that almost changed U.S. history. The president's two-week tour of New England was to finish in Pittsfield, Massachusetts. A gala reception was planned in his honor at a local country club. Thousands of people jammed

Pittsfield's Park Square to watch the presidential carriage pass by.

Roosevelt's carriage was traveling on South Street alongside a packed trolley car headed to the country club. Suddenly, the trolley sped up. Apparently, the driver was attempting to move in front of the carriage, to arrive at the reception in advance of the president. At the base of Howards Hill, the trolley smashed directly into the carriage throwing Secret Service agent William Craig under its wheels and crushing him to death. As for the President, he was thrown face-first into the dirt street, then rushed into a private home across the street for medical treatment. One of the horses was killed, and the trolley car driver was arrested and jailed for six months.

Injuries to Roosevelt included leg and facial wounds. A few days after the accident, an abscess developed in his leg. He underwent surgery and was confined to a wheelchair for several weeks.

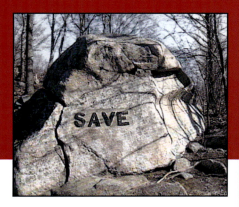

Tom Smith and the words of Dogtown.

Years later, the president would state that this accident altered the state of his health for the rest of his life. Yet today, few people outside of Pittsfield have ever heard of the incident that almost killed a president.

The Messages of Dogtown

Gloucester, Massachusetts, is best known for its ties to the sea. But a few miles inland from the town's famous harbor, the woodlands hold a curious sight. Historian Tom Smith is happy to serve as guide.

"This area of Gloucester came to be known as Dogtown because after the Revolutionary War, it was inhabited by old widows and pensioners," Smith begins. "As they died off, one by one, and the houses began to collapse, all that was left were the dogs running wild. And so the whole section became known as 'Dogtown.'"

Roger Babson, a self-made millionaire who founded Wellesley's Babson College, was drawn to these woods.

"Roger Babson, as a gift to his hometown of Gloucester, acquired all of Dogtown Commons in the early 1920s," Smith continues. "He donated it to the town—lock, stock, and barrel—as a wildlife preserve. Also, he had a unique style of conveying his theories on life. Instead of writing an autobiography, he came to the flat rocks of Dogtown and carved inspirational messages for the people who wandered through here to see and reflect upon."

And so, to this day, visitors to Dogtown can take in Babson's oddly haunting advice. "Courage," reads one inscription. "Be Clean," reads another. And on they go, each with a sound and practical message: "Keep Out of Debt." "Be on Time." "Help Mother."

"It's really a unique collection," Smith remarks, while sitting atop "Never Try, Never Win." "It's everything you ever wanted to read on a tea bag, but you don't have to go to the trouble—they're all carved right on the rocks here."

Ben Craig and the Buck monument, Bucksport, Maine. The leg, and the legend, continue.

Revenge from the Grave?

Bucksport, Maine, on the banks of the Penobscot River, is named for Colonel Jonathan Buck. By all accounts, Buck was a Revolutionary war hero and well-respected town father who served for a time as a local judge. As one legend has it, he once sentenced a woman named Ida Black to be hanged, and she swore a witch's curse against him. Another legend claims that Ida Black was burned at the stake upon Buck's orders. Ben Craig of the Bucksport Historical Society knows the details of the second version of the story.

"When the fire got going real good, one of her legs burned off and rolled toward the colonel. He had to jump to get out of its way," Craig says. "Somebody picked it up and threw it back on the fire and everything burned up. That probably would have been the end of it, but when they erected this monument the outline of a woman's leg appeared on it."

Craig points to the very obvious markings on the Buck monument. "Looks like a sock to me. Or a stocking hanging on a line."

According to legend, the marking first appeared on the anniversary of Buck's death, and no amount of sandblasting or chemicals can remove it. Today, the monument is an offbeat tourist attraction. "Traffic's been blocked because of it," Craig reports, "usually Massachusetts drivers!"

Research shows no evidence that Colonel Buck ever sentenced a woman to death. What's more, granite commonly has flaws like this one. "It's too bad Colonel Buck is being remembered because of this leg," laments Craig, "when he was a great enough man to be remembered in his own right."

Yet the leg, and the legend, continue.

Losing His Mind

In recent years, the Vermont town of Cavendish received a great deal of publicity as the hideaway of Alexander Solzhenitsyn. But more than 150 years ago, Cavendish was known for the freakish accident of Phineas Gage.

Sandra Stearns, president of the local historical society, knows the story well. "Phineas Gage came to Cavendish in 1848. He was about 25 years old, and worked as a construction foreman putting the railroad through Cavendish. His main job was as a tamper for the blasting operation."

"This bar that I'm holding here is similar to the rod Gage would have used for tamping. It would have been made of iron, weighing about 13 pounds. As I under-

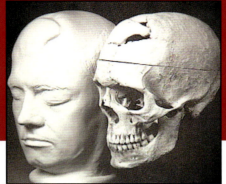

Dr. John Harlow, the skull of Phineas Gage, and Sandra Stearns demonstrating the gruesome details of the injury.

stand it," Stearns explains, "they put the black powder in, and with his bar he'd lightly tamp the powder. After that, they'd pour sand on top of it, and then he'd firmly tamp that. But apparently he dropped his bar into the powder, and it made a spark on the rock and it blew the powder off."

Stearns knows all the gruesome details: "The bar went sailing through the air. It went in through the cheek here and, as I understand it, it didn't hit the jawbone. It was above the jaw, up behind the eye, and out the top of his head on the opposite side. It stuck right through his head."

An iron rod, three-and-a-half feet long, had blown through the face, brain, and skull of Phineas Gage—and he survived! John Harlow, a physician, tended to Gage and later wrote, "I dressed his wounds. God healed him."

After just four months the holes had healed, and it was thought that Gage was recovered. "So he applied for his old job," Stearns relates, "but the company wouldn't hire him again, because he had so changed."

With part of his brain missing, he was Phineas Gage no longer.

"They said before, he'd been a good worker. He'd make plans and carry them out." But no more. "When he came back he was irritable, not reliable," Stearns reports. "And they said—and this is a quote—'He used the grossest profanities' they'd ever heard. And he *never* swore before. They wouldn't give him his job back."

Phineas Gage spent the next 12 years wandering and unhappy. In 1861, he died suddenly, following a severe convulsion. Dr. Harlow convinced the Gage family to donate the skull and tamping iron to medical science. Today, they belong to the Harvard Medical School.

Fort Blunder

At the Canadian border, along the Northwestern shore of Vermont's Lake Champlain, stands Fort Montgomery. Although no battles were fought here, Fort Montgomery certainly deserves its place in history. For this is where the United States made the mistake that earned this place its nickname, "Fort Blunder." Historian Howard Coffin knows why.

"There was ample reason to build a fort here on Lake Champlain. The British had invaded the fledgling nation in 1775 and 1776. And then came the War of 1812, and again the British came south, down Lake Champlain and also down the land," Coffin explains. "So, come 1816, the decision was made—quite logically—to build a fort

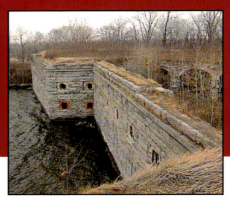

Howard Coffin (left), and Victor Podd (far right), at the remains of Fort Montgomery.

right here on the border, in case the British had any more ideas about invading the United States. The problem was, after the construction was well on its way, they found out they were building this 50-cannon fortress in *Canada*! They didn't do the survey until 1816, and lo and behold, it's in Canada. So construction stops immediately. It wasn't until 1842 and the Webster-Ashburton Treaty that this becomes United States property again."

Today there's a new twist to Fort Montgomery. This U.S. property happens to be owned by a Canadian. As Victor Podd tells us, he bought the fort 20 years ago, and now he's trying to sell it.

"We put it up for sale in *Unique Homes* with an asking price of $2.5 million. We've advertised in Tokyo; we've advertised in London. We've had several inquiries, but nothing too serious in nature," Podd reports. He's ready to be a little more flexible. "Today, we're comfortable saying that our asking price is between one dollar and $2.5 million."

UPDATE: The Phineas Gage case is now a classic in neurology textbooks and continues to fascinate medical researchers. In 1978, two University of Iowa neurobiologists were given permission to do a "virtual autopsy" on Gage's brain. Using computers, they were able to determine that the accident damaged the portions of the frontal lobes that control rational decision making and the processing of emotion. "Gage's story was the historical beginnings of the study of the biological basis of behavior," claims one of the researchers.

In 1998, on the 150th anniversary of the accident, the town of Cavendish hosted a festival and scientific symposium to honor Phineas Gage. Visitors could purchase reproduction tamping irons and t-shirts emblazoned with Gage's skull. On the more serious side, neurologists from as far away as the Netherlands gathered to view x-rays of the skull and share research on the frontal lobes of the brain. (They also had an opportunity to watch our Chronicle segment, which was made available at the request of festival organizers.)

As for Fort Blunder: Victor Podd has passed away, and the property is still owned by the family. They are not actively trying to sell, but would certainly entertain serious inquiries or offers.

HAUNTING LOCAL LEGENDS

Wherever there is history, there are ghosts. And New England, it appears, has plenty of both. In fact, the supernatural is often a matter of local pride; New Englanders love to tell and retell local legends of haunted schoolrooms, demon sightings, and ghostly guests at the local inn. Just in time for Halloween of 1996, Peter Mehegan explored some of these legends as he traveled the uncharted territory of haunted New England.

Haunted Hartford

Hartford, Vermont, was the scene of one of the nation's worst railroad disasters. Back in 1887, the midnight Montreal Express was on its way through Hartford when, at 2:00 A.M., a rail cracked and the train's rear car jumped the tracks *and* the roadway alongside the tracks.

"When it got to the bridge, it pulled, fell over the bridge, and pulled the sleeper cars with it," says Vermonter Steven Marshall. "In those days, the cars were heated with coal stoves and kerosene lamps were used for lighting. The cars caught on fire and burned, which set the bridge on fire, and the bridge burned and collapsed," Marshall recounts. At least 31 people died and scores were

Courtesy: Dartmouth College Archives

injured. "As you might expect, something like that would produce ghosts," Marshall says, referring to the rebuilt bridge. "It is haunted."

A retired Defense Department physicist, Marshall now has a new title. He's been called a "tour guide into another dimension."

"The barn is where they took the wounded and the dead and that's haunted," he states. "I keep hearing stories that they can't keep animals in that barn. The animals will panic or some of them will refuse to be pulled into the barn."

But that's not all. "There's another story of a man who walks on top of the trestle, wearing a conductor's uniform," Marshall says. "People occasionally see him, and also people come by

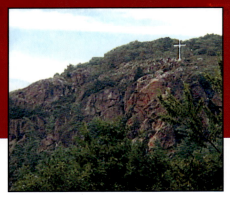

Steven Marshall, left, Maiden Cliff, right, and waitress, Peggy Jackomino, far right.

here at night and see the headlight of a train."

He recites a ballad written shortly after the disaster, called "The Montreal Express":

"One I never shall forget, was of little Joe McGrett,
Who was with his father on that fatal train.
Although wounded by a fall, still he heard his father's call
And to free him from the wreckage he tried in vain.
'It's no use my boy,' said he, 'for there is no help for me.'
Then the cruel flames around him curled.
Little Joe began to cry when his father said goodbye.
'We'll meet again up in the other world.'"

"And that," Marshall concludes as he stands beside the tracks, "happened right here."

The Maiden Cliff of Maine

With its picturesque harbor and imposing mansions, Camden is one of Maine's most popular tourist destinations. On a ridge overlooking the town is Mount Battie.

From its summit, visitors can take in striking views of town, harbor, and coastline. But few ever venture behind the ridge to a place known as Maiden Cliff. Even fewer know the origin of its name.

It was a windy day in May of 1864 when the French family decided to go for a picnic on the cliff. Evil, it seems, was in the air. A gust of wind flung 11-year-old Elenora French from the cliff and she fell to her death. To this day, a tall, white, wooden cross marks the fateful spot.

But some say that tragic day was not the end of the little girl. Over the last century, strange visions have been reported on and near Maiden Cliff. In the 1930s and 1940s, dozens of people claimed to have seen Elenora's apparition, enveloped in the warm winds of springtime. The last recorded sighting was 1976, but there are still those who keep their distance from Maiden Cliff.

Ghosts a la Carte

Numero's Restaurant in Windham, New Hampshire, looks like a friendly Mexican restaurant. Indeed, it is that, and much more. According to the owners and staff, this unassuming eatery, with its pool table and well-worn bar, has been haunted for years. Waitress Peggy Jackomino has seen the proof with her own two eyes.

"She was here," Peggy says, pointing to the spot behind the bar where she first saw the ghost. "We were diagonally looking at each other, and this slight mist came right out of the wall and came right through the

Chef Paula Phillips, left, points to where a pot fell off the wall; Numero's restaurant; the haunted attic, above.

bar in front of us, and went out over to the Budweiser sign. She walked right through or floated right through and disappeared right into the wall."

Peggy has heard rumors about the source of the spirit. "We know that in the beginning it was a restaurant and reportedly had little rooms upstairs, where ladies of the evening conducted their business," she says. "They claim it is one of the ladies of the evening who is haunting this place."

Upstairs in the attic, Peggy's descriptions can give you the shivers. "This is where you hear a lot of walking and boards moving," she claims. "It's actually footsteps that you hear—like high heels clicking."

Manager Laverne Cassidy recalls the ghost's latest visit. "Recently, we were talking about her and said that she hadn't been around for a while, so we thought maybe she had gone." No such luck. Cassidy points to a child's booster seat resting on a shelf. "All of a sudden, this seat comes flying off the shelf! It lands on the floor and we start laughing and say, 'Well, she didn't want us to think she was gone, so she showed us she's still here!'"

Apparently, ghosts get hungry. At least that's what chef Paula Phillips thought, after she was paid a visit in the kitchen. "I was standing here doing my prep work when, out of the blue, the pot fell off the wall," Phillips recounts. "I have no clue how that happened. The hooks are straight up, so there's no way a pot can just fall off the wall."

Back at the bar, Peggy Jackomino adds, "You'll put something down and you can actually see it sometimes just move a little bit, with no explanation. You can see it moving, but there's nobody there."

UPDATE: Want to buy a restaurant? Numero's newest owner, Shelly Beshara, just can't take it anymore. And she has owned the place for only a few months. Before making her decision to close, Beshara consulted psychics for help. They recommended a frank and forthright chat with the ghosts. After one cook spoke up, asking the ghosts to leave in peace, a small piece of wood loosened from the wall and fell directly into her hair.

Just days before we called to check in, Beshara had given up and closed Numero's for good. "Things have gotten out of control, it's just too weird in there," she declares. Now the restaurant is on the market, available at a fair price to a brave soul. "If it doesn't sell, I'll take my losses," Beshara sighs. "I just want to be done with the place."

SUGAR HIGH

The welcome sound of sap running. The sweet smell of steam on the rise.

And then, that very first bite. In 1999 Chronicle traveled to the Berkshire hill towns for a taste

of an early spring ritual: sugaring season. We had to hurry—the season lasts just six short weeks.

"Sugaring season is sort of when winter and spring are battling for control," explains Tom McCrumm of Massachusetts Maple Producers. "What we need for sap to flow is nights with temperatures in the low 20s, and warm, sunny days in the mid-40s. We don't want it too warm; we don't want it too cold."

In Massachusetts alone, sugarhouses number close to 250. Boyden Farm in Conway still does things the old-fashioned way: a team of oxen is led from one maple tree to the next when it's time to collect the sap.

Sugaring has a long history. McCrumm speculates on who first savored the sweetness. "Indians were tapping trees when the white man first arrived," he says. "My thought is some early human found a sapsicle (McCrumm's word for frozen sap) hanging off a tree branch and ate it and found that it was wonderful."

Maple sap is colorless and essentially tasteless. "Ninety-eight percent of the water is boiled off. What's left is pure maple syrup," says McCrumm. The color and grading of finished syrup depends on timing. "As a rule of thumb, lighter syrup is earlier in the season and darker syrup is later."

And what to do with all that syrup? Spread it on pancakes certainly, but why stop there? There's maple candy, maple cream, and a New England classic: "sugar on snow," which is served, believe it or not, with a side of pickles and Saltines. "What you want to do is drizzle the syrup over the snow," a waitress at Gray's Sugar House demonstrates. "It caramelizes and

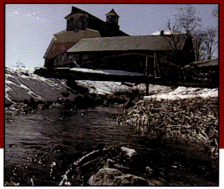

Tom McCrumm, the sugarhouse, and a tempting New England treat, syrup on snow.

makes a sort of taffy. The pickles and crackers cut the sweetness."

There's nothing quite like breakfast in a sugarhouse. Gray's, in Ashfield, draws more than 6,000 diners during its six-week season. They come for sugar on snow, pancakes, French toast, waffles, and more. But be prepared: the waiting line at Gray's is legendary. "We've been in line for probably an hour and fifteen minutes," one hungry customer sighs. "We do this every year. We pick out a Saturday and we tough it out."

The wait, we're told, is worth it, not just for break-fast, but for the entire experience. "This is really what a sugarhouse should look like," another customer adds. "The old maples, the winding stream—really typical of old New England."

Sweet Site

For a complete listing of Massachusetts sugar houses, along with general information, recipes (including sugar on snow), and instructions on producing your own syrup, visit the Massachusetts Maple Producers Web site, www.massmaple.org.

The Line

William Gray, the eldest of three generations at Gray's Sugar House, knows just how seriously people take their sugar. He tells the story of one diehard maple syrup lover who was nine months pregnant. She was at the front of the waiting line when she went into labor, Gray recalls. "She'd be darned if she was going to miss her pancakes and maple syrup, so she sat down, ate her breakfast, and then left to deliver the baby."

ROADSIDE CURIOSITIES

Call them odd, or call them art. They're commercial buildings and signs from a bygone era, with a style and a sense of whimsy all their own. Today, many of these examples of "architectural advertising" have disappeared. In 1999, Mary Richardson got behind the wheel to search for New England's remaining roadside oddities.

Towering Termite

If you've traveled along Interstate 95 through Providence, you've probably seen the big blue bug. It's hard to miss this termite of epic proportions. One way to find out just how big it is is to climb to the rooftop with New England Pest Control's Dave Pontes.

"The bug is 58 feet long, and weighs 4,000 pounds," Pontes reports. "The legs are 12 feet long, the antennae are 8 feet long, and the bug is 928 times the size of a real termite."

Dave explains that the termite was created in 1980 to herald the company's relocation. Few could have predicted the fame that would follow. The big blue bug has made an appearance in the movie *Dumb and Dumber* and on "The Oprah Winfrey Show." When Denver's new airport commissioned a mural of the United States, they chose the loveable termite as Rhode Island's lone symbol.

Then there are the daily traffic reports. "The accident is so many miles from the bug, north of the bug, south of the bug," Dave intones. "Everybody refers to it as the big blue bug. But you know, he does have a name . . . ."

Dave pauses, making you ask.

"Nibbles Woodaway," he delivers. "A very appro-priate name for a termite."

On holidays, Dave and his colleagues like to have some fun with Nibbles, and he has photos as proof. "At Christmas he had 5,000 lights wrapped around him," Dave boasts. "On the Fourth of July, he had a big Uncle Sam hat and whiskers. One Halloween, we gave him a witch's broom and hat."

Milking It

Raynham, Massachusetts, is home to another classic roadside delight: the Milk Bottle Restaurant. In the 1920s, six of these 40-foot bottle-shaped eateries were scattered around New England. Today, three are left standing—including the popular bottle beside Boston's Children's Museum. In Raynham, the exterior could use a coat of paint, but inside, the food remains as it always has been: good, cheap, and plentiful.

Manager Karen Dutra says that old-timers usually order only *after* they've shared memories with the waitresses. "They tell us, 'Gee, I remember coming here when I was little,' or 'I remember my Dad taking me when it was on Old Coach Road,'" she says.

Karen Dutra at the Milk Bottle Restaurant.
Nibbles celebrating the holidays.

The big cactus.

As for new customers, Dutra wishes she had a dollar for every time a child has asked whether there's really milk inside the bottle.

Plastic Pasture

The Boston area's best-known roadside attraction has to be the cactus at Hilltop Steakhouse in Saugus. Standing 68 feet tall and made with 15 miles of neon, some have said the cactus is to Saugus what the Eiffel Tower is to Paris.

But such fame doesn't come without concerns. "We often worry when we have heavy rains and storms and hurricanes," shares Hilltop's Leonard DeRosa, "but it's built 30 feet into the ground, so it will never be top heavy."

When it comes to roadside attractions, the Hilltop is actually a two-fer: the restaurant's herd of fiberglass steer, grazing on the front lawn, is campy—and beloved.

"We do about 45 weddings a year," DeRosa reports. "We just had a bride who insisted on having her picture taken on top of the steer before the ceremony. "

Spatial Relations

Warren, New Hampshire, in the heart of the White Mountains, is an ordinary New England town. Ordinary, except for one thing—a Redstone rocket, said to be the only privately owned missile in the world, stands in the town square.

According to Warren resident Bud Pushee, the town convinced NASA to donate the rocket as a way of making science come alive for schoolchildren, and as a tribute to New Hampshire-born astronaut Alan Shepherd.

"It's a tourist attraction," says Pushee. "It's part of history, it has integrity to the state. And besides, we don't have a whole lot around here," he adds. "Sixty-five percent of this town is natural forest."

UPDATE: Nibbles's dress-up days have dwindled. Though he still wears 5,000 lights at Christmastime, he no longer sports Fourth of July or Halloween attire. Costs, says Dave Pontes, have become prohibitive.

CIRCUS FIRE TRAGEDY

*July 6, 1944, was a hot day in Hartford, Connecticut. But families wither-
ing in the heat and worried about loved ones fighting overseas had a distrac-
tion at hand. The Greatest Show on Earth was in town—the Ringling Brothers
and Barnum & Bailey Circus. A crowd assembled for what they expected to be a
day of fun; instead, they became unwilling participants in one of the New England's
greatest tragedies. Chronicle told the story in the winter of 2000.*

Eight thousand men, women, and children came to see
the show. Among them: seven-year-old Elliot Smith, his
twelve-year-old sister Joan, and their mother Grace.
Elliott remembers the day well.

"It was so terribly hot that we decided to go in the
tent to get out of the heat. My mother had general admission tickets, but she decided to upgrade them to reserved
seating, so we went into the tent and waited for the show
to start," Elliot recalls.

"It was my first circus under a tent, and my last."

A wild animal act had just finished its performance.
The Famous Flying Wallendas prepared to follow. In a far
sidewall of the tent, behind the bleachers, a small flame
crawled up to the canvas roof, where it found fuel in the
paraffin and gasoline, used as waterproofing materials.

Stars and Stripes

Band leader Merle Evans spotted the flame, and cued his
band to play "Stars and Stripes Forever," the signal to
circus workers of an emergency. Then the crowd began to
notice. To Elliot's horror, "a huge tongue of flame went up
the far side wall. Then after that, everybody stood up."

A panicked Joan Smith ran to the top of the tent.

"I said to my mother I'm going to go up. I got up
on top of the chairs and I jumped from chair to chair, until
I got up to the top of the tent. I grabbed hold of the canvas and the canvas gave under my weight and then I
dropped."

Joan fell to safety. Elliot Smith and his mother joined
the crush trying to exit a nearby stairway.

"My mother took me by the hand and she said that
the ushers were directing people out so she went the way
the ushers were directing us. Unfortunately, that funneled
the whole crowd to the stairway over the runway and it
was a bottleneck."

In the confusion, Elliot lost his mother's grip.

*Donald Anderson (left) and
Elliot Smith (far right).*

"All I could hear was screams and the clattering of all these folding chairs being knocked out of the way as the people made a mass panic exodus."

Eight thousand people had less than five minutes to escape. Thirteen-year-old Donald Anderson used a knife to cut his way through the tent.

"I shoved the knife in, ripped it down, made an aperture and got out," Anderson says. But many of those fleeing, especially children, fell in the hysteria and were trampled to death.

"A lot of kids got trampled, because survival of the fittest is pretty strong. I picked up this little girl, maybe three, and I brought her outside."

Help at Last

Elliot Smith was one of those knocked down in the mass panic. Other people tumbled on top of him. Then the burning tent collapsed.

"I was immobilized by these people on top of me. I

An enduring mystery of the Hartford Circus Fire is the identity of one of the unclaimed victims, a girl who came to be known as "Little Miss 1565." Hartford arson investigator Rick Davey studied the records in the 1980s, and determined that the girl was eight-year-old Eleanor Cook of Southampton, Massachusetts, whose brother Edward also died in the fire. In 1991, the Cook family moved her body from the mass grave in Hartford to their family plot.

But author Stewart O'Nan, in his book The Circus Fire, *argues that the bodies were so horribly burned that many victims were misidentified, and that the mystery of this little girl's name will never be solved.*

could see the reflection of the fire on the ground directly in front of my face, heard the screams," Elliot recollects.

"To me laying there with my face against the ground it was eternity. At first everyone was screaming and praying and then that quieted down and then I heard male voices and the sounds of water from a fire hose and then a splash of water hit me and it felt awfully good so I called for more. And then I had to say, 'Stop you are going to drown me.' Then I could feel the weight being lifted off me, once, twice, and then a third time the weight lifted off, fell back."

Twenty-four-year-old William Cieri was one of the first firefighters on the scene. The horror of what he saw stays vividly with him today.

"There was one little boy there who was about nine years old and his hands were just like this, like he was praying," Cieri remembers. "Even today I can see these people . . . ."

Hope at the Hospital

A total of 167 people, mostly women and children, died in the Hartford Circus Fire. Many more suffered horrible injuries. Grace Smith, severely burned on the shoulders and head, found herself on a stretcher in a crowded hallway of Hartford's municipal hospital. She later told her daughter Joan, how she saw the doors to a nearby elevator open. "A gurney came out, and she felt compelled to raise herself up," Joan said. "And it was her brother."

Elliot had survived, shielded by the layer of dead bodies pressing upon him under the tent. But he had been badly burned as well. For the next five months he would undergo painful reconstructive surgery. He's kept one souvenir from that difficult time, the autograph book he had in the hospital, signed by the nurses and fellow patients.

Elliot reads from the book a note from his favorite nurse. "To an old Meanie from an old Meanie, best of luck. Becky Beckshaw, RFD#1, North Wilmington, Ma." He remains grateful: "She was my angel. She could get me to do things I didn't want to do or endure things that were difficult to endure," he says.

Although Elliot never saw his nurse again after leaving the hospital, he later named one of his children Becky.

Six of the fire victims were never identified, and were laid to rest in a cemetery in Hartford. The monument by their side reads, "Their identity known but to God."

In 1950, a drifter named Robert Dale Segee, who had a history of arson and mental illness, confessed to starting the fire. But authorities declined to prosecute him for lack of sufficient evidence. Although an exact cause of the fire was never determined, several circus managers were convicted of involuntary manslaughter in connection with the tragedy. And, ultimately, the circus paid out some four million dollars in claims to victims and their families.

UPDATE: Elliot Smith's quest for Becky Beckshaw was solved by Chronicle viewer Karen Keough. The woman Elliot knew as nurse Becky Beckshaw was actually Valerie Violet Bieksza of Tewksbury, Massachusetts. A nurse during World War II, she volunteered to relocate to Hartford to attend victims of the circus fire.

Violet married and had three children. In 1967, she died of a brain aneurysm at the age of 44.

AUTUMN SPLENDOR

When it comes to setting up our Main Streets & Back Roads series in autumn, one question needs to be answered immediately: Where's the color? If we have a show set in rural New England during the fall, and there's no blazing red, orange, or yellow leaves as a setting for our stories, we feel like we've failed. Luckily, our staff is resourceful, the various foliage hot lines are helpful, and we usually manage to find at least a few technicolor trees.

Sometimes the background becomes the foreground, and our story is the foliage itself. We've done stories on the biochemical dance of chlorophyll and carotenoids, tracked down the real places behind the pretty postcards, and boarded the leaf peeper buses as they make their rounds. In the fall of 2000, we captured the region's annual show in high definition television.

The glory of a New England autumn is as spectacular as it is fleeting. Timing a trip to see it at its "peak" is an iffy proposition: go too early, and you get dull green with intermittent tints; go too late, and you get muted shades at best, bare trees at worst. In our 20 years of chasing foliage, we've found one place to be the most reliable in delivering consistent color—New Hampshire's Kancamagus Highway.

The "Kanc" stretches 34 miles across the White Mountain National Forest, following the Swift River from the east and the Pemigewasset River from the west. All along the road there are lookouts to view the show. And, according to Alexis Jackson of the White Mountain

National Forest, the reviews don't disappoint. "People come from all over the world to see the "Kanc," Jackson says. "We've seen folks from Great Britain and Germany, Australia, China, all parts of the Far East, Japan—we get them from everywhere."

Foreign foliage fans can turn to *Yankee Magazine*'s two foliage sections in September or October, or surf onto NewEngland.com, *Yankee*'s Web site. Senior Travel Editor Carol Connaire says inquiries about the foliage schedule come in from all over the world, especially from Europe.

"When I am interviewed, people ask, 'Is it going to be any good?' And I say, 'Well, in the past thirty-four

years that I've seen it, it hasn't been bad!'" Still, Connaire says predicting nature is a risky business. "It's really a gamble. You never know exactly when it's going to peak. That's fun for us because we live here, but for visitors it gets a little tense."

Photo Synthesis

It can also get tense for anyone selling film along the foliage trail. You have to be fully stocked, because everybody wants a picture to take home. Amateur shutterbugs even dream of taking a snap so great that *Yankee* might want to publish it. Picture Editor Tripp Mikich is the man who passes muster on all those rolls of film.

"It's just been done so much you feel like, 'God, I've seen this before,'" Mikich admits. But he does have a few photo tips for first-time photographers. "The first thing to do is look and let yourself really see what you're looking at. Take a few minutes; that's what you're there for," Mikich advises. "Look for other elements in the landscape, something else you could bring into the picture: a little bit of fence, or the classic gravestone in a graveyard, or a bit of branch that's hanging down in front. These types of things can make it more interesting. If it's just an amorphous bunch of colored trees, usually it's not going to look exactly as you're seeing it."

Picture Perfect

Are those places whose images adorn calendars, postcards, and book jackets the Edenic outposts they appear to be? East Corinth, Vermont, where Mary Martin runs the village store, is one of those places. "Nothing's as nice as the postcards, but it's probably as close as you can get in real life," Martin says. "If it's not perfect, you can just walk into the woods and then it's perfect."

Photographers often walk up nearby Picture Hill and shoot the world-famous view of East Corinth.

Peacham is another one of Vermont's most photographed towns. Karen Stawiecki of the Peacham Store has a theory about what brings the Kodak and celluloid crowds to certain Vermont towns. "You take away the utility poles and it looks like it did 200 years ago."

That's true of East Orange and East Topsham, Tunbridge, and Reading. Reading's Jenne Farm has been called the most photographed farm in the world. Over in Waits River, people line up on October days to get their version of the village's signature shot: the town church, flanked by barns, with a wooded hill behind.

Hitting the Peaks

Of course New England offers no shortage of places from which to view the fabulous foliage. It might cost you the price of a toll road and a few rolls of film. Or you could splurge on a few nights away from home. But if you live in New England, you owe it to yourself to experience the foliage firsthand in a deeper way than from behind a windshield. After all, no place does it better.

"In New England, we get the best colors because of our climate here and the diversity of tree species we have," explains Massachusetts Forest Health Specialist Alison Wright. "Each tree species will turn a known set of colors. Red maple turns red, sugar maple turns yellow and orange, so as we go down the list we will have a variety of colors all the way down to the purple range."

Such a gift, delivered to our doorsteps, is too glorious to ever be taken for granted.

Fall Foliage Hotlines

Vermont: 802–828–3239; www.vermont.com
New Hampshire: www.newhampshire.com
Massachusetts: www.mass-vacation.com/foliage.html
Maine: 800–777–0317; www.state.me.us/doc/foliage

ISLANDS & BYWAYS

MAIN
STREETS
&BACK
ROADS.

VERMONT'S SNOW ROUTE

The American Automobile Association calls Vermont's Route 100 the state's most scenic highway. In winter, it earns another title: Vermont's Snow Route. Chronicle's Mary Richardson took us along for a tour in March of 1998.

Vermont's Route 100 starts at the Massachusetts border, tracing along the spine of the Green Mountains as it travels 181 miles north to Canada.

The road is also known as the "Skiing Highway," because it passes by eight major ski areas in the state. The Grande Dame of these is Mad River Glen in Waitsfield, which celebrated its 50th anniversary in 1998. In an age of snow guns, Mad River Glen depends on the natural stuff, with limited snowmaking and mostly ungroomed terrain. Or, as one devotee told us, "Mad River is skiing in its original form."

It also depends on a unique cooperative to stay open. Since 1995, skiers have been able to buy shares in the area, giving them a say in its running along with reduced lift ticket rates. Shareholders say the cost ($1,750 per share in 2000) is a small price to pay to preserve this old-fashioned way of skiing. Mad River marketing director Eric Friedman says he knows "a lot of people who don't have health insurance but they have shares in Mad River Glen."

Jake Burton

Snowboarding, as you might expect, does not fit in with the Mad River Glen philosophy; boards are banned. That's ironic, since the man most identified with the sport lives just down the road in Stowe.

Jake Burton couldn't even qualify for a credit card when he began Burton Boards in 1977; 20 years later his Burlington-based company led the market with $150 million in sales. But Burton still has high ambitions—he tries to go boarding at least 100 days a year.

Post-Ben and Jerry

If winter sports are not your favorite leisure activity, you could always consider a working vacation of sorts. Rochester's Liberty Hill Farm off of Route 100 takes in guests who are invited to pitch in with the daily dairy chores. If that's too strenuous, Waitsfield's Lareau Farm Country Inn features draft horses available for a ride.

Lareau Farm is also the world headquarters of American Flatbread. Chicago transplant George Shenck, a pizza aficionado who found Vermont's pizza pies lacking,

Flatbread, flakes, and fiery sauce.

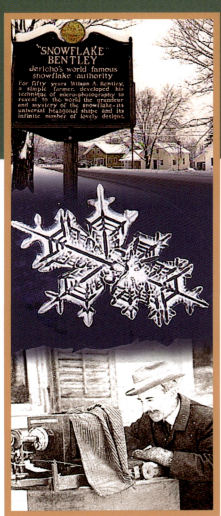

Courtesy: Jericho Historical Society

started the company in a vacant barn on the Lareau farm. Now its gourmet flatbreads are shipped around the country to health food stores and groceries.

In fact, Route 100 shows many signs of PBJ (Post-Ben and Jerry) Syndrome. Scores of entrepreneurs in Waterbury, home of the ice cream kings, hope to capitalize on Vermont's pure and natural image to make their own splash in the food business. For Joseph Brent, aka Jo B, it's a line of hot sauces that he hopes will capture the public palate.

When it comes to family businesses, Stowe boasts one of the most famous. The Trapp Family Lodge is the legacy of Georg and Maria von Trapp, who brought their children to Stowe in 1939, after the events depicted in the movie *The Sound of Music*. There are 29 von Trapp grandchildren, but just one—Elisabeth—keeps the family's musical flame alive. A Waitsfield resident, she's a contemporary folk singer who's released two CDs.

Snowflake Bentley

While on the "Snow Route," many people take a short detour to remember a man obsessed by those little ice crystals. Jericho, Vermont—a few towns west of Route 100—was the home of Wilson "Snowflake" Bentley. Around the age of 19, Bentley decided to devote his life to proving the theory that no two snowflakes are alike.

In 1925, he wrote, "Under the microscope, I found that snowflakes were miracles of beauty; and it seemed a shame that this beauty should not be seen and appreciated by others."

Using a camera fitted with a microscope, he photographed thousands of flakes over a period of 50 years, wrote a book about his work, and lectured across the country.

Today, the historical society operates a small museum to honor the man who took a closer look at a tiny part of our world, and changed the way we see winter.

WASHED ASHORE *on* BLOCK ISLAND

The Nature Conservancy calls Block Island one of the 12 "last great places" in the Western Hemisphere. Chronicle visited twice in recent years, in the summer of 1989 and the spring of 1995. On both visits, we spent time with two men who personify the island's charm and endurance.

Block Island formed about 12,000 years ago, carved out by a glacier that also shaped Long Island, Martha's Vineyard, and Nantucket. The result is an island that looks like a pork chop—seven miles long and three miles wide—sitting a dozen miles off the mainland. Native Americans from the Manissean tribe were the first human inhabitants; they named their home Manisses, or Island of the Little God. Dutch fur trader Adrian Block came ashore in 1641, leaving his name behind him when he left. Twenty years later, English settlers fleeing the unyielding ways of the Puritans made a more permanent settlement here.

Block Island survived as a farming and fishing community until just after the Civil War, when steamship service introduced the first tourists to the island. In the late 1800s, a large number of Victorian-style hotels were built. Block Island became one of the country's most popular resorts, eventually earning a reputation as the "Bermuda of the North."

But the tourist heyday didn't last for long. Cars killed the steamship trade and visitors opted to go to more convenient places. Block Islanders went back to farming and fishing, and by the 1950s many of the hotels had gone to seed. It was around that time that an East Greenwich, Rhode Island, couple named Joan and Justin Abrams began to take sailing vacations to Block Island. During Chronicle's 1989 visit, Joan told Andria Hall that it was Justin's idea to turn their vacation spot into a workplace.

"My husband thought that it would be fun for us to be able to spend most of our days on the beach, and the kids would have something to do," Joan recalls. "But it ended up that for three years I never *saw* the beach."

The Abrams bought their first property—the 1661 Inn—in 1969. But they had greater ambitions: to buy and restore one of the grandest Victorian hotels—the Manisses—which sat boarded up and in disrepair. In 1972 it became theirs, for $10,000, and the prospect of months of work.

"The Manisses was a very rundown hotel," Joan says. "Every time I'd go by it after we bought it I'd shud-

Joan Abrams, the Manisses,
and Dr. Peter Brassard.

der, because I never in a million years thought that we would be able to restore it back to what it is today."

But restore it they did. Daughter Rita remembers her first impressions. "There was no question that it looked like it was coming down," Rita recalls. "And we did have to take down the back half of the building, which had the ballroom."

The Abrams renovated all 17 rooms, and gave each one a name: the Princess Augusta, the Palatine, the Palmetto, the Pocahontas, and so on. Honeymooners checking in for their inaugural voyage might not want to know about the inspiration for those names—each one is a ship wrecked off Block Island. However, to ease the anxiety, a hospitable surprise awaits in each of the guest rooms: a complimentary decanter of brandy.

Moped Madness

It's not ships that wreck nowadays on Block Island; it's mopeds. The roads are winding, narrow—and crowded, says O.J., a former New Yorker turned island taxi driver.

"In my opinion this place is vehicular anarchy," O.J. declares. "You can't go by the book here. You have roads that are normal roads, and on these roads you have trucks,

you have cars. You have mothers with babies, 300 scooters, 2,000 bicycles, all the cars that can come on the ferry. But somehow it works."

And sometimes it doesn't. Dr. Peter Brassard came to Block Island's Medical Center in 1986. Mopeds, he tells us, are the bane of his existence.

"Fifty percent of all ambulance calls—all ambulance calls—in 1994 were due to moped accidents," Dr. Brassard states. "If Block Island was an amusement park—and many would argue that it is—and you had a ride in an amusement park that was responsible for a hundred busted or maimed bodies every year . . . it wouldn't take a Nobel Prize winner to shut that ride down."

The rides haven't been shut down, but maybe the riders have slowed down. Police recorded 40 moped accidents in 1998; the number declined to 27 in 1999.

Most travel guides recommend biking or walking as the best way to get around the island. Hikers can explore the Greenway—a network of trails over 12 miles long—a communal project of the Nature Conservancy, private property owners, and community groups. Many visitors go to see the Mohegan Bluffs, 200-foot cliffs named after the losers in a battle won by the Manisseans.

Nearby is Southeast Lighthouse. And it's nearer than

Lighthouse keeper Lisa Nolan.
and Captain Bob Cottle, far right.

it used to be, because in the early 1990s, it was in danger of not being at all. Lisa Nolan knows that better than most, because she lived in the lighthouse. "It was perched atop the bluffs, which, as far as we know, have always been eroding at a rate of about 3 feet a year," Nolan says.

Islanders rallied to move their beloved beacon before it became driftwood at the bottom of the bluffs. It was a 2,000-ton brain teaser, but with the help of a retired engineer from Washington state (ably assisted by hydraulic jacks, travel beams, and Ivory soap for lubrication), the lighthouse relocated from here to there. It returned to service in August 1994; the campaign to completely renovate its interior continues today.

Captain Weather

Another familiar island sight is Bob Cottle, cruising the Block in his 1950 Ford, dubbed the "White Whale." To several generations of New Englanders, he was Captain Bob, an artist and storyteller who hosted several children's television shows. He began coming to the island in 1948, bought land across from Crescent Beach a few years later, and built a waterfront home, all for the cost of about $2,800. In the winter of 1988-89, he became a full-timer,

puzzling some of his friends.

"People say 'What do you do in the winter on Block Island?' Well, my wife and I have a funny little thing—at least we think it's funny," Cottle says. "In the evening, after you've been active all day long, and you get a little bored, you get in the car and you drive downtown to see if the Coke machine is lit."

Somehow that story didn't sound right. And, on our 1995 return visit, Captain Bob admitted there were other attributes that drew him to Block Island. The real reason he wanted to live right in the middle of the Atlantic Ocean, just about dead center between the Rhode Island coast and Montauk Point, was more complicated. He was, he confessed, a weather nut.

"I think it's great to see it savage," Cottle proclaims. "I like to see weather happen."

He liked it so much, in fact, that he purposely put his oceanfront home at risk. "We've got all this glass facing northeast because when I built the house in '61, I wanted to see storms coming in! And boy do we see them. Yahoo!"

His favorite weather of all? Fog, which reminds him of one of his favorite stories, the one about the tourist, the fog, and the fisherman.

"... and the fisherman said pppttt (spits), 'Ma'am,

*The "White Whale",
and Fred Benson, far right.*

that ain't fog; that's just a little mist rising up from the lobster bait. But I'll tell you what fog is. When you come down here in the morning and you look out, and you can't see the end of the dock. You start walking along and you put your hand out in front of you, and when you run into your hand—that's fog!'"

Mr. Block Island

While Bob Cottle is a visitor who fell in love with his adopted home, Fred Benson is a man literally adopted by the island. Benson was born in Boston in 1895 and abandoned by his parents. As a young boy, he was sent to Block Island to live with a foster family. During his lifetime, he has worked as a commercial fisherman, taxi driver, businessman, coach, Chamber of Commerce president, and teacher, among other occupations. When we met him for the first time, he was the island's deputy registrar of motor vehicles, at the age of 95.

Benson's life has been so intertwined with the community that he became known as Mister Block Island. That reputation only grew when he won the lottery in 1975, and donated his $50,000 winnings to create scholarships for local children. Asked why he was so generous,

his answer was simple: "If there is any good that I can do or any kindness I can show, let me do it now for I shall not pass this way again."

In 1994, Fred Benson was forced to move to the mainland for health reasons. But when he came back for his 100th birthday, he was greeted by a dockside reception of about 500 people, more than half the island's year-round population. His reaction was heartfelt: "No President has ever received a greater reception than I have today. God bless you."

U P D A T E : In 1996, Fred Benson died at the age of 101. But his memory is preserved for islanders and tourists alike at Fred Benson Town Beach, just minutes away from the ferry landing. Bob Cottle left the island he loved, in 1997, to move to California. He died there after a stroke in 1999. The "last, great place" of Block Island is the poorer for their passing.

Want to visit? Ferry service is year-round from Point Judith, and seasonally from New London, Montauk, Providence, and Newport. Call Block Island Ferry, at 401–783–4613, or visit www.blockislandferry.com. New England Airlines also flies daily to the island from Westerly, R.I. (800–243–2460).

MOHAWK TRAIL

The first officially designated scenic highway in Massachusetts, a section of Route 2 has been dubbed the Mohawk Trail. It is a thoroughfare best taken at cautious speed, especially on Deadman's Curve and the Hairpin Turn. Chronicle traced its path in the fall of 1994.

Drive through the center of Orange, Massachusetts. Head on out Route 2, past the mill town of Erving. Now, check your brakes and your wallet—you're about to motor onto the Mohawk Trail.

Why check your brakes? Because this 63-mile stretch of Route 2, running from Greenfield by the Connecticut River to the New York border near Williamstown, requires strict attention from drivers. Take Deadman's Curve, for example—very slowly.

Right by the town of Drury, heading westbound, the road takes a steep decline. Many a trucker has miscalculated just how steep. There is a 200-foot drop for those who fail to negotiate the turn. Sometimes the result is a fatality. More often, the truckers' load goes over the bank. Stan Brown, who owns a garage a mile from the site, says he's seen it all: "Loads of lime, diesel fuel, cattle, candy, beer, slate—anything you name has been over there."

And Deadman's Curve is not the only challenge for motorists on the Mohawk. In Clarksburg, there's the Hairpin Turn. At one time, a gift shop sat perched on the cliff at the bend of the turn.

That changed in 1958. Lyn Morris's uncle was working there that day. "My Uncle Don saw this tremendous truck hurling down and dove into the men's room," Morris says. "And while they were checking to see the extent of the damage another truck came right through and did the exact same thing and that was the end of the building. It completely ruined it."

But that was not the end of the gift shop. It was rebuilt behind a rock ledge to protect it from any more runaway trucks. And that approach worked—until 1982. That's when a fuel truck rammed the cliff and exploded, killing the driver. Lynn Morris and her husband rebuilt in the same location, turning the gift shop into a restaurant, The Golden Eagle. Morris says there have been only minor scrapes since then. Perhaps the message has gotten out—take it slow on the Hairpin Turn.

Merchandising—Mohawk-style

There is one time of year when speed is definitely not a problem on the Mohawk. In foliage season, you couldn't go fast if you tried. Leaf peepers crawl along to catch

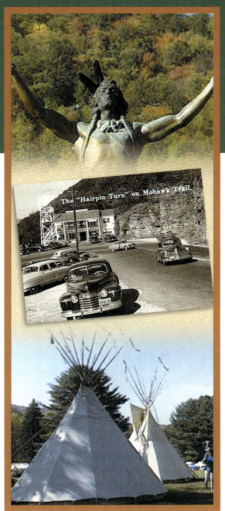

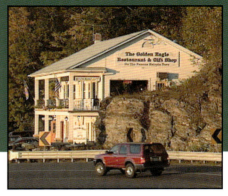

Intertribal pow-wows and perilous purchasing on the Hairpin Turn.

every glimpse of chlorophyll. And roadside gift stands beckon the roaming shopper, adding the color of red brake lights to that of sugar maples.

Whether or not the concept of a roadside stand was born on the Mohawk Trail is debatable, but there's no doubt that it was perfected here. But that's fitting, since it's always been a trade route, starting with Native Americans. The Mohawks and the Pocumtucks, among other tribes, came to fish the salmon falls on the Deerfield River.

It's believed that the trail was part of a much larger route that ran from the Great Lakes to Cape Cod. You can still see traces of that Indian heritage in roadside monuments. And, every fall at the Indian Plaza in Charlemont, there is a series of intertribal pow-wows.

The Mohawk Trail evolved from a footpath, to a horse and cart track, to, finally, a road for automobiles.

In 1914, the trail was designated the Bay State's first scenic highway. Stan Brown, whose father opened his garage beside it in 1923, has photographs showing the old way of keeping a business open in winter: shoveling the road by hand!

The highway's heyday came in the mid-1950s. It was the major east-west thruway, and in the fall cars would wind bumper to bumper along its length. The opening of the Massachusetts Turnpike in the late 50s stole some of that thunder, and traffic flow is not what it once was.

There are many attractions along the route, and over the years, Chronicle has visited most of them: the Bridge of Flowers in Shelburne Falls; Old Deerfield's collection of pre-Revolutionary homes; the Hoosac Tunnel, a 19th-century railroad passage that cost 200 lives and $15 million in the building; and Whitcomb Summit, the highest point on the Mohawk Trail.

VINEYARD HOSPITALITY

Chronicle has visited Martha's Vineyard many times, years before Bill Clinton made it his summer vacation spot, and well before celebrities like Ted Danson, Diane Sawyer, and Spike Lee helped rev up real estate prices. We've met authors and artists, farmers and fishermen, summer people and seasonal workers. One story we've explored over the years is the bond between African-Americans and the island.

The Scribe of Oak Bluffs

It's the fall of 1984, the time of year when the year-rounders begin taking back their summer playground. The tourist dollars help make the winter months affordable, but the tradeoff is congestion, traffic, and demanding visitors that can try the locals' patience. As the island saying goes: When it comes to summer people, some are people—and some aren't.

Peter Mehegan is on his way to visit author Dorothy West. On this warm October afternoon, she's feeling like the hostess who was happy to throw a party—and even happier to see the guests leave.

"We are glad to see the summer people come and we are glad to see the summer people go, because we feel we have the island to ourselves again and we see people," West says. "In the summertime, your next-door neighbor may be in the store but

Dorothy West

you don't see her. Now you do and you take time. You take time here to talk to people."

Dorothy West talks to a lot of people, no matter what the season. That's because she is a columnist for the *Martha's Vineyard Gazette*. Her beat: the town of Oak Bluffs.

"I have always written for the *Gazette*, I mean for years and years and years," West says. "And then the day that they called me and asked me if I would do the Oak Bluffs column, I said, 'You are not going to believe this but I was going to call you and ask you if I could do a piece every couple of weeks!'"

At the age of 77, West retains the enthusiasm of youth, leaning forward to emphasize her points and breaking frequently into infectious laughter. She is a humble, gracious hostess, making it easy to forget the role she played in American literature.

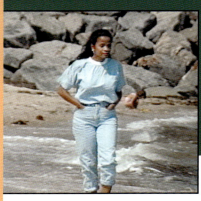

*Dorothy West and Chronicle's
Peter Mehegan; resident
Andrea Bolling Burnett, far right.*

West was born in Boston in 1907, the daughter of a freed slave turned successful businessman. She wrote her first story at the age of 7; by 14, she had won several literary contests.

While still in her teens, she moved to Harlem, and began to circulate with a group of other young black writers, including Langston Hughes, Richard Wright, Countee Cullen, Zora Neale Hurston, and others. Their work became part of the Harlem Renaissance, an outpouring of African-American prose, poetry, music, and art in New York City during the 1920s.

At the same time as she was making her mark in Manhattan, West continued a love affair with the Vineyard, one that began at the age of three with annual summer trips.

"When we were children, coming down here on the train, you got to, I think it was Falmouth, and you began to smell the sea," she recalls. "And even though we were carefree children, something came over us. And you knew that this place was—this place *is* different than any place in the world."

In New York, West wrote short stories, published two magazines, and worked for the WPA Federal Writers Program. In the 1940s, when many of the principals of the Harlem Renaissance had dispersed to other parts of the country, West moved to Oak Bluffs full time, where she wrote her first novel, *The Living Is Easy*, about the black middle class in Boston.

Despite good reviews for her first book, no publisher accepted her second novel. As a writer, she was not surprised. Rejection was part of the territory.

"I began writing many years ago, and I had an excellent agent, one of the best agents in New York," West explains. "And he would send the story and then he would send me the rejection slip. And the rejection slip sounded just like acceptance—until the end."

Unlike the publishing world, West says the Vineyard gives her comfort and support, producing a perfect atmosphere to create.

"There's peace here, a great deal of peace."

And—she says—racial harmony.

"This island is really a microcosm of how people, races, get along," she maintains. "I've never been to any black person's party where there were not whites and the same for a white person's party. Therefore, you are closest to your nearest neighbor. It doesn't make a difference if she's black or white."

Birth of a Resort

Unlike many summer resorts, however, there is a better chance your neighbor might be black in Oak Bluffs. In 1989, Chronicle's Andria Hall looked at some of the reasons why the community became a vacation destination for middle—and upper—class black Americans.

The resort town that is Oak Bluffs today grew out of a summertime Methodist religious retreat established just before the Civil War. Worshippers came and camped out in canvas tents for the revival style meetings; eventually, the congregants who returned year after year replaced the tents with gingerbread-style, pastel colored cottages.

The religious atmosphere attracted a black man named Charles Shearer. Shearer, a former slave, had been a college teacher and a head waiter at Boston's Parker House Hotel. He and his wife, Henrietta, bought two homes and land in the area known as The Highlands. They then invited friends to join them in the summer.

By 1912, the Shearer cottages had become a summer inn, one of the few to welcome minority customers, giving many black visitors a place to enjoy their first experience of the island. And these were no ordinary visitors: Actor Paul Robeson; Reverend Adam Clayton Powell, Senior; Congressman Adam Clayton Powell, Junior; Singer-actress Ethel Waters.

And the tradition continues, although the names have changed, and the visitors stay in their own homes, rather than renting rooms. Power broker Vernon Jordan. Film director Spike Lee. Former presidential cabinet member Louis Sullivan. For him, there is a thread that connects the era of the Shearers to the present community.

"It really, I think, is a microcosm of blacks who have distinguished themselves," Sullivan states.

A well-dressed, middle-aged woman sitting on a boat in the harbor agrees. She says the Oak Bluffs community is highbrow, and proud of it.

"My husband stood on the shore for the first time in 1983. He's from Oklahoma but he went to Harvard Law School. When he looked up, he said, 'Half of the blacks from my Harvard Law School class are on this beach. We're coming back.'"

"The stability of the black community here is what we really enjoy," says an older man in the same group. "It's not a bunch of different people. The same kind of people come here every year and it works."

"It sounds elitist, and I suppose it is in a way," chimes in a second woman. "And I think there's something to be said for that."

Judge Herbert Tucker first came to the island in 1926. Now a year-round resident, he remembers the resort

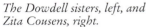
*The Dowdell sisters, left, and
Zita Cousens, right.*

as "almost primitive." In his time, he's seen more development, and more people, every year.

The Dowdell sisters—Mildred Henderson, Ruth Scarville-Bonaparte, and Kathy Allen—pitched in together to buy their home in 1956. At the time, it was a financial stretch—almost $10,000.

"When we first bought this house we had to find a house that was convenient in case we didn't have a car," Henderson explains. "We were all buying homes back in New York and we didn't know whether we'd be able to afford another car to be here. So we had to find a house where we'd be able to walk to the beach and walk to town."

Ruth remembers the Oak Bluffs of those days as a very different place.

"It was gorgeous and it was underpopulated. Very few people . . . maybe 6,000 summer residents," Henderson recollects. "Our children were very young, four and three. And we could turn them loose, they could walk into town. They had never done this before."

For Andrea Bolling Burnett, spending summers in Oak Bluffs in the 1960s meant going to the beach with the unusual nickname.

"We used to call this beach the Inkwell. And I assumed the reason we called it the Inkwell was because

there was a lot of seaweed and so the ocean was black," she says. "It wasn't until I got older, into my early teens, that I was told the reason they called it the Inkwell was because this is where all the black people went to swim."

Asked if that was considered an affectionate term, Bolling Burnett replies, "Oh, definitely, and now it has taken on a life of its own."

Zita Cousens sees the growth in Oak Bluffs from two vantage points. As the owner of Cousen Rose Gallery since 1979, she's seen her sales of art increase over the decade, making her gallery a destination for locals and tourists alike. As a resident, she's also seen a quiet place lose some of its peace.

"Sometimes I do worry about it," admits Andrea Bolling Burnett. "The people who grew up here, and the people who live here and buy homes here, I think really have a stake in the community," she says. "I think people who are more transient don't have that same commitment."

Kathy Allen says her family won't take the money and run—even though that $10,000 investment is worth many more times than that today.

"Never. This is one house that will be handed down from generation to generation. We never know what the young folks will do but as far as we're concerned we'll never sell it no matter what."

Chief Joe Carter and the public he protects. Elaine Weintraub, far right.

New Chief in Town

Flash forward to the autumn of 1998. Oak Bluffs' popularity has grown by leaps and bounds. Some residents worry that the community feeling they have nurtured is in danger of disappearing. The job of maintaining their peace of mind falls to the town's new police chief, who's left the big city, Boston, to make a new life on the island.

"We have a little bit of everything that is fine about New England here in Oak Bluffs. I consider it the hub of the island." He sounds like the president of the Chamber of Commerce, but the man singing the praises of his new town is Joe Carter, the recently arrived police chief.

Before he came to the island, he was Deputy Superintendent Joe Carter of the Boston Police Department, the highest ranking black officer and the youngest on the command staff. Then the Oak Bluffs job became available. Carter, a summer-home owner for ten years, jumped at the chance for a change of scenery, and a different type of policing.

"It's night and day," he muses. "Our problems are mostly family related. Most folks know each other who get involved in incidents. That's a big difference in comparison to the types of crimes that they deal with in the city of Boston on a day-to-day basis."

Policing the Party

But there was one big city-type problem that Carter did have to deal with right away. In recent years, the Fourth of July celebration had been bringing in a younger, louder crowd that put off some residents and vacationers. In his first days on the job, it was Chief Carter's challenge to respond to the old-timers and deal with the troublemakers, all while making the new visitors feel as welcome as previous tourists.

His solution: mounted police.

"An officer on a horse can see a whole lot more than an officer on the ground when you have thousands of people congregating," Carter explains.

He also imported Boston plainclothes officers to keep track of any visiting gang members.

"It was documented that they were here. There was no secret about that," he says. "Our goal was to have the experts here on the ground to be able to assist the officers here who don't have the experience in identification."

Some took offense, saying the police appeared ready for a riot. But the result, says Carter, speaks for itself: an incident-free Fourth.

"There is a new chief in town, if you will. Law enforcement is a lot more progressive."

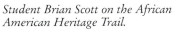

Student Brian Scott on the African American Heritage Trail.

Honoring the Heritage

Although the Vineyard was a welcoming place for African-Americans for generations, one high school teacher did not think their contributions were properly recognized and set out to rectify what she saw as a wrong. Chronicle covered her efforts in the spring of 2000.

"There are places on this island that are noted for their beauty," says Martha's Vineyard High School history teacher Elaine Weintraub. But Brian Scott, one of Weintraub's students, knows that there is pain behind the postcard beauty. "Not many tourists realize that all these fields were cleared by slaves."

Weintraub and her students are trying to increase awareness of their island's complete history through the African American Heritage Trail. Established in 1997, the trail marks 16 sites that tell stories of struggle and triumph.

In Chilmark, the trail stops at the fields once worked by Rebecca Amos, an African woman from Guinea who survived the Middle Passage. She worked as a slave on the farm of Revolutionary War hero Colonel Cornelius Bassett until he died, setting her free. She later married a Wampanoag man named Elisha Amos, and inherited his home upon his death.

Another stop is at the Chappaquiddick homestead of William Martin. Weintraub and her class identified Martin as the unnamed black whaling captain mentioned in island oral histories. Working jointly with NAACP archivist Carrie Camillo-Tankard, the team made another discovery: that Martin was the great grandson of Rebecca Amos.

Weintraub and her students are spearheading a drive to raise money to buy Captain Martin's old homestead and turn it into a living museum. But with the price of real estate high, that will take a lot of funds. The group is also restoring abandoned grave sites for people of color.

UPDATE: Dorothy West finally got her second novel, *The Wedding*, published in 1995 with the help of a famous friend, Jacqueline Kennedy Onassis, who was an editor at Doubleday at the time. A third book followed, *The Richer, the Poorer: Stories, Sketches, and Reminiscences*. West died in 1998.

Gallery owner Zita Cousens is now selling art to the children of the people who first shopped her gallery in 1979.

As for the Fourth of July celebration, police say the "family" feeling of the holiday has re-asserted itself.

OLD KING'S HIGHWAY

The Old King's Highway is better known to most people as Route 6A, and is sometimes confused with its far more congested cousin, Route 6. Once the only route across Cape Cod, the highway strings together towns whose names ring with history: Barnstable, Yarmouthport, Brewster, and Orleans. From beginning to end, Chronicle took a "royal tour" of this scenic road back in 1993.

The first town on Old King's Highway is Cape Cod's oldest, Sandwich. It's where Howard Crowell has been running Crow Farm for 63 years. These days, Howard's son, Paul, works alongside him, on farmland that's been feeding Cape Codders for nearly 300 years.

As he rinses just-picked lettuce, Howard remarks, "People enjoy getting something fresh that was cut today and sold today and will be eaten today. All your supermarkets have produce grown in California or Florida; it's been on the road for a week, sitting in a fridge, losing taste."

Another green spot in Sandwich is a briar patch made famous by Thornton Burgess. Burgess, a Sandwich native, was a naturalist and author of more than 15,000 children's stories and 170 books; *The Adventures of Peter Cottontail* is his best-known work. Seven years after Burgess's death in 1965, the town of Sandwich purchased the briar patch and surrounding land.

Today, the Sandwich Conservation Commission manages the 52-acre Briar Patch Park. Peter Cottontail would be pleased.

Hiding Out Back

Further down the highway is Jack's Outback, a restaurant that's hard to find and wants to stay that way. Catering to locals, it's tucked behind Route 6A because "that way, we can keep away all the New Yorkers," owner Jack Smith explains. "The Chamber of Commerce prefers that we're back here anyway, so there are no tourists in our 'line of fire,' so to speak."

Jack lives upstairs from the restaurant. Early morning customers used to throw rocks at his window to get him out of bed and behind the griddle. "Eventually, we gave keys to the customers," Jack discloses. "So now, whoever gets here first puts the coffee on and turns on the stove. By the time we get here, some customers have eaten, paid, and gone."

Jack Smith, the Parnassus Book Service, and Gavin McLeod at the Cape Playhouse.

Books off the Beaten Track

After more than 42 years, neatnik Ben Muse is learning to live with the clutter inside his Yarmouthport book shop, Parnassus Book Service. Parnassus is no ordinary bookstore. It's a combination of new and used books, some of them rare, priced anywhere from five cents to a few thousand dollars. All are organized—pretty much—by subject.

"I've been criticized because I don't have signs to tell you where to go," Ben remarks. "Well, I think if you're intelligent enough you'll roam around. After all, the sense of discovery is what it is all about."

The building itself is a treasure worth discovering. Built in the 1840s as a general store, it sits less than ten feet from the road. From the porch, it's easy to imagine a time when horse-drawn carriages were the only traffic along the Old King's Highway.

Cape Curtain Call

Opening night jitters aren't the only thing pressuring performers at the Cape Playhouse in Dennis. There's also the illustrious history of this stage.

"When you get on the boards, when you get on that stage, you *know* who your predecessors were," explains Gavin McLeod, best known for his roles on *The Mary Tyler Moore Show* and *Love Boat.* McLeod has played the Cape Playhouse three times. "It *does* something to you," he says. "You say, 'Now I belong to this fraternity.'"

The fraternity includes Tallulah Bankhead, Basil Rathbone, Bette Davis, Shirley Booth, and Henry Fonda, who all found their way to a theater once described as "five miles past nowhere."

The Playhouse got its start in 1927 when, before the invention of air conditioning, Broadway all but shut down for the summer. Raymond Moore, a businessman and a dreamer, gambled on three acres in Dennis.

"Let's face it," says set designer Helen Pond, "actors do like to act. They like to appear onstage. And when they couldn't do it in New York because of the heat, they'd come here. They'd go anywhere."

Pond, herself a New Yorker, finds that she's spending more and more of her time on Cape Cod. "This area is really very special," she proclaims. "We have it all set so that we can work in the morning and go swimming at noon. You can't do that in New York."

U P D A T E : Jack may not be pleased, but word is getting out: in 2000, Jack's Outback was awarded a "Gold Medal" for "Best Mid-Cape Breakfast" by *Cape Cod Life* magazine.

MOUNT DESERT ISLAND

Three million people visit Maine's Mount Desert Island in the summertime, stopping into the shops and restaurants of Bar Harbor, hiking through Acadia National Park, driving up Cadillac Mountain for the view, or rushing to catch the ferry to Nova Scotia. Chronicle has visited in the craziness of peak tourist season, but in the fall of 1996, Peter Mehegan decided to see what goes on when the crowds go home.

French explorer Samuel Champlain gave the island its name in 1604. As he sailed by, the stark, barren tops of the mountains struck his imagination. Searching for an appropriate name to convey the wild sense of loneliness, he dubbed the area Mount Desert Island.

Of course, there's nothing deserted about the island in June, July, and August. But there is a little more room to move in the autumn. Bikers can pump their way up Cadillac Mountain without looking over their shoulders for an oncoming SUV. And a beginning sea kayaker like Peter can get out in the waters of Bar Harbor without worrying about a boat bearing down on him. Ben Thellwell, a guide with National Park Sea Kayaks, says autumn is a good time to learn the sport. "The trip that we generally run is a four-hour trip," Thellwell says. "I would say with that trip, 99 percent of the people are first-time paddlers, and they pick it up really quickly."

Timed by the Tides

If you live on Mount Desert Island, you learn something else very quickly: you need to pay attention to the water conditions. That's especially true if you live on an island off the main island, as does Jack Perkins, a longtime television correspondent, with NBC, PBS, and now, A&E on his resume. He knows his way around a plane or train schedule. But on Bar Island, it's the tides that rule his life. At low tide, it's no problem to get out to his home. But, at high tide—it's boat, or bust.

Bar Island also has no public electric service. So, Perkins makes his own, with solar cells on the roof and a bank of batteries in the basement. "We use electricity very sparingly," he explains. "We have adapted our lives and probably use much, much less electricity than most people in most situations. But you quickly realize that all those things that we always considered necessities are not really necessary."

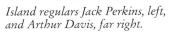

Island regulars Jack Perkins, left, and Arthur Davis, far right.

In fact, making adjustments was the reason the Perkins family moved from Los Angeles to Maine. "It was as drastic and total a change as we could make," he declares. "I believe that every soul needs at least once in a life time, and maybe more frequently, a total and drastic change in geography, psychology, philosophy, and everything, and so that is what it represented for us."

The move to new surroundings has expanded the horizons for Perkins. His latest passion is photographing nearby Acadia National Park. He's since published a collection of pictures and poetry, *Acadia: Visions and Verse.* His photos have also been featured in a local gallery.

Plastered Pub

There are certainly a lot of galleries in town. But there are other kinds of displays as well. In one, hundreds of old signs cover every available space. License plates are plastered all over the place. The forum for this exhibit is Geddy's Pub on Main Street.

Owner Arthur Davis claims Geddy's is more than a place to get a beer. It's a pub with a purpose: preserving artifacts from all around Bar Harbor. It's evident that many came from places where security is lax and signs are loose.

"Some of the signs may have just appeared from places in the middle of the night," Davis admits. "I guess that did happen in the past."

But he insists most signs are brought to him voluntarily to add to the collection. Sure, there was an unpleasant incident concerning a National Park Visitor Center sign that hung outside the pub. Several park rangers visited, resulting in a subsequent un-hanging of said sign. But, Davis says the Geddy's philosophy is clear: all Park Service signs go back to the Park Service. And if you've lost a sign, and find it at Geddy's, he'll gladly hand it over.

Purple Menace

There is one thing on Mount Desert Island the Park Service would love to see disappear. It's a plant called purple loosestrife, originally imported from Europe because of its beauty. You see it in summer as it flowers, and the result is quite pretty as it fills in wetlands with a pastel topping. But the effect is far from benign, as it chokes off other plants, cattails, and grasses. If you pull it up, it returns even stronger. So how do you fight this alien invader? Park Service botanist Linda Gregory says herbicide is the weapon of choice in Acadia. But there are places where mercenaries are employed. "Certain insects have been brought over from Europe, which feed just on this plant and on the roots and some of the flowers," Gregory explains.

Skip Byars-Basso, left,
Linda Gregory, center, and
Richard Walls, far right.

Trial by Fire

Purple loosestrife is certainly a pressing problem. But this community has survived more serious challenges. In the fall of 1947, it almost burned to the ground. Richard Walls, who was fourteen at the time, remembers it was a very dry year and the trouble began with the burning of rubbish at the dump. "When it got burning, it went underground," he recalls. "When they thought they had it out, they left it and it sprung up a quarter of a mile from where they put it out."

Sixty-mile-an-hour winds whipped up a wall of flames five to ten miles long, and sent the fire burning along Shore Road toward the village of Bar Harbor.

"All the way around the west side of the town it burned all the summer houses pretty much right down to the ground," Walls says.

The west side was the rich side of town, home to mansions, hotels, and inns. The fire burned for ten days, destroying more than sixty properties. Just when the village itself was encircled, the wind shifted, and Bar Harbor proper was spared. But the damage was clear.

"The only thing they saved was chimneys," Richard Walls remembers. "There was a whole town full of chimneys—nothing else on them."

Road Kill 101

Few of the millionaires behind those burned-down "cottages" rebuilt, bringing an end to an era. Several of the structures that did survive were turned into inns or bed and breakfasts. But one became a school—the College of the Atlantic. C.O.A. is known for its marine ecology program, but it's also interesting to see the taxidermy department in action. Instructor Skip Byars-Basso conveys the fine art of turning road kill into natural history display.

"Once the skin is taken off, it's just like taking your coat off," he maintains. "You take the skin off. It's all cleaned off. All the meat that is left in there is cleaned out. Then you make something that goes back into the body to keep it in shape."

It's clear that recycling in all its forms is the Bar Harbor way. If an animal turns up dead on a local roadway, turn it into an opportunity for education. If the tide makes your house inaccessible, use it as an experience for personal growth. So if you want to make this wild and beautiful place your home, you'd best have a talent for turning necessity into virtue.

Along the MOLLY STARK TRAIL

Travel New England, and you can find a highway named after a King, a trail bearing the name of a Native American tribe, and numerous bridges and tunnels named after politicians. But it's rare to find a road that calls attention to a woman. Chronicle's Mary Richardson found one in Vermont in the winter of 1999.

It's called the Molly Stark Trail: Route 9 in southern Vermont. Stretching 46 miles between Bennington and Brattleboro, the road is dotted with nods to its namesake: the Molly Stark Inn, the Molly Stark State Park, and the Molly Stark Elementary School, among others.

So who was Molly Stark? The anticlimactic truth came from Tyler Resch of the Bennington Museum. "Molly Stark was probably nobody who deserved to be remembered in history books," Resch contends.

Ah, but what about the Bennington Battle Monument, which stands tall at the edge of the Old Bennington district? It commemorates the defeat of the British in the battle of Bennington in 1777. The general commanding the victorious troops? John Stark, Molly's husband.

The story begins to make sense at a stone monu-

General John Stark

Courtesy: Bennington Museum

ment near the New York state line. On it are inscribed the words of General John Stark, words he spoke to his troops just before taking on the British. "There are the redcoats and they are ours. Or this night Molly Stark sleeps a widow." History tells us Molly did not sleep a widow that night; in fact, the victorious general returned to his Molly and their New Hampshire home by way of an old Colonial military patrol path. That path, twisting up and down through the Green Mountains, was the forerunner of today's Molly Stark Trail.

Not Your Average Mall

Obviously, these Stark facts deserve further investigation. But first Mary makes a detour to go to the mall—the Woodford Mall. Adam Adamski is the mall's owner. But he has no Gaps, Sears, or Wal-Marts on the premises.

Adam Adamski, above.

The Woodford Mall, ten miles east of Bennington, is the oddly named headquarters of Twin Brooks Tours and the Woodford Snowbusters—the largest snowmobile club in America.

Adamski says he has 5,000 members in the club. From Woodford, sledders can find their way onto thousands of miles of groomed trails, running through remote forest land all the way up into Canada. Mary doesn't have time for a journey that long, but she does strap on a helmet to make her maiden voyage. The verdict? "Whoo!"

Power-up

A few miles from Woodford, machines of a quieter nature dominate the high hills of Searsburg—200-foot turbines that generate electricity for the Green Mountain Power Company. Dave Sweet is the caretaker of this powerful brood, and he has but one request: take care not to call his charges windmills. Windmills pump water out of the ground. These machines put juice into your home.

Sweet says his job, which seems like a mountaintop version of a lighthouse keeper, has some fringe benefits as well. It keeps him outdoors, where he can take in all the gorgeous sunrises and sunsets he can handle.

Returning to the investigation of Molly Stark, what better place for R and R (research and reminiscing) than at a B&B: the Molly Stark Inn in Bennington. Innkeeper Reed Fendler acquired a rare drawing of Molly when he bought the inn and over the years he's also heard most of the stories about the woman herself. He relates that Molly and the General had eleven children, and that their descendants are today spread all over the world.

A Town on the Move

Perhaps the expatriate Starks took Route 9 out of town. After all, it was the first road to traverse Vermont from east to west. And it's still the best way to get across southern Vermont. That's good news for all those Molly Stark inns and gift shops and diners and so on, but it's been bad news for the town of Wilmington, Vermont. Wilmington

Reed Fendler and Mary with Molly Starks' portrait, center, and Skip Morrow, far right.

is home to the only traffic light on the entire Molly Stark Trail; subsequently, it owns the only continuous traffic jam. Cars and trucks traveling east, west, and south converge on the little village at the intersection of Routes 100 and 9. Sometimes the backup can stretch close to an hour.

The state and federal governments have spent hundreds of thousands of dollars looking into highway bypass plans. But Wilmington resident Skip Morrow—an artist, author of *The Official I Hate Cats Book*, cartoonist, and musician—has what he thinks is a better idea.

"When I first thought of it I kept it to myself actually, for about a year, thinking that people would think it a little odd," he admits.

Skip's idea? Move the town, not the road. People didn't call the idea "odd"; they called it "ridiculous," "absolutely nuts," and "crazy." Skip's proposal involves moving about a hundred historic buildings from downtown in the village to an open area on the shore of Lake Whitingham. And he says there's precedent for the move. In the 1830s, the town of Wilmington actually *did* relo-

cate, from nearby Lisle Hill to its present location. The villagers made the move to take advantage of the commercial possibilities presented by a new road—the Molly Stark Trail.

Will Wilmington move? Well, it's an option that will be considered by state and federal officials, along with two possible bypass routes. No one expects anything to happen for at least a decade. But, on a road with a Revolutionary heritage, you never know.

Before we leave the Molly Stark Trail—and tale—we pass along one bit of gossip. It comes courtesy of Marlboro gallery owner Harold Makepeace. "The rumor was that Molly Stark was Ethan Allen's girlfriend," Makepeace whispers. "And evidently she was quite a live wire."

So it may have been more than patriotic fervor that made Molly so eager to run messages from her husband to Ethan Allen, Vermont's famous Green Mountain Boy. It's a story that can't be confirmed, but it certainly adds to the mystery of Molly.

The Original "On the Road"

A hand-me-down car and a fondness for Maine. That's what kicked off one of Chronicle's most popular series. Peter Mehegan first went "On the Road" back in 1987. Since then, he and the old Chevy have logged more than 25,000 miles together along the Maine coastline.

While all of the trips have been accident-free, they have not been incident-free. One winter, a family of mice took up residence in the Chevy's upholstery. A few Januarys later, the heating knob broke off in Peter's hand, on a morning that registered 20 degrees below zero. Road salt and old age continue to curse the car, and rust is an ever-present enemy. But with professional maintenance on the Chevy and tender loving care from Peter, this TV twosome will be "On the Road" for many years to come.

Here's Peter's presentation of his very first Down East adventure and, as they say in Hollywood, the "backstory" to the old Chevy.

Chronicle went on a search for the perfect vehicle to take us upcountry, to find New England stories. It couldn't be just any vehicle; nothing flashy would do. It had to be understated and laid back. In keeping with the character of New England, the search ended in my own backyard.

There, partially hidden by weeds, was a 1969 Chevy. The car had been cherished by a departed aunt, but had recently fallen on hard times. Specifically, it wouldn't move, due to a sick transmission.

But at Chronicle we'll spare no expense to get the story. So, with the boss's somewhat skeptical permission, the old Chevy was towed from the weeds to Wayne Robbins's Garage in Cohasset. Wayne allowed that the car was salvageable; her problems were nothing that a little cash wouldn't cure.

"Go ahead, Wayne," I said, "The boss wants this car to run again, well enough to carry me upcountry." If Wayne had his doubts about that, he didn't say anything.

Harlan Wallace, left, speaking to Peter, and John Gould, center. Far right, Wallace's labs greet Peter.

He just went to work.

A few weeks later, the old Chevy was back on the road again. Wayne had done his work well. We had made it upcountry, all the way to the great state of Maine.

A Town by Any Other Name

Maine has many charms. Among them are its place names: Christmas Cove, Pretty Marsh, Sunshine, and—our first stop on this visit—Friendship. It's a town of about 800 people, seven miles south of Route 1, near Rockland. The main industry is lobstering.

Friendship appears aptly named. A visitor to Harlan Wallace's lobster dock can count on a friendly greeting from Wallace's two Labrador retrievers.

Harlan himself is a man of few words. The sign on his dockside shanty is as Maine as the ruddy faces of the fishermen. "Harlan's Corner Store," it reads. "Known in New York. London. Paris."

When asked if he fishes himself, Harlan replies, "Used to. Fished for twenty-two years."

Does he like it better ashore?

"At times," is all he says. People from outside Maine—from "away," as Mainers put it—sometimes describe the natives as aloof and standoffish. John Gould, one of Friendship's most prominent citizens, disagrees. "Easiest people in the world to get acquainted with, but you don't want to jump in 'til you're ready to swim," Gould says emphatically. "This delusion of aloofness—it's created by people that approached somebody and asked the *wrong* question, and got the *right* answer!"

Gould dispenses his wisdom from his coveside home just outside Friendship Village. His essays on Maine have been syndicated worldwide for decades by *The Christian Science Monitor*. In fact, Gould was writing Maine humor when humorist Marshall Dodge was still in short pants. Gould says his material is all around him: it's his neighbors.

"I made the crack one time that in Maine, we didn't write books, we lived them," Gould chuckles. "You went to your grange meetings, you went fishing, and you went out each fall after your deer. And this, that, and the other happened. And finally, you *had* a book—you didn't *write* it. And when the pile was big enough, you sent it to a publisher. There's a lot of truth in that."

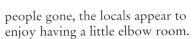

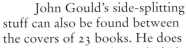

Sheila Fowler, right, and her restaurant, Sheila's Shanty, above.

John Gould's side-splitting stuff can also be found between the covers of 23 books. He does his writing in a six-by-eight hideaway in his woodshed.

"The typical state of Mainer? There's something to that," Gould pronounces. "We perhaps are laconic, and careful in our words. I think we tend to be logical positivists. There's the story of the fella who says, 'There's a white horse,' and the other fella says, 'Well, it looks so from this side.' This might be a touchstone of Maine humor."

Gould recommends a stop at Sheila's Shanty on the way out of town for a steaming bowl of chili.

Sheila Fowler used to shuck clams for a living. She got bored, and opened her lunch stand just outside of Friendship Village. "I wanted to work for myself," she says as she tends to a sizzling hamburger. "And I didn't want to do clams anymore, and I like to cook, so here I am."

On this winter day, business is slow at Sheila's place—just a few locals. But they're more than willing to pass the time with a stranger, and lunch and a cup of coffee go well with the conversation. With the summer people gone, the locals appear to enjoy having a little elbow room.

"This is when we do our heavy work, in the wintertime," one diner relates. "Because in the summertime, we want the business open to keep it going."

Suddenly, Sheila's culinary skills are put to the test. Customers begin arriving in droves. Harlan Wallace's wife, Charlene, and a coworker from the cannery. A scattering of hungry locals from the docks. And two newcomers from Rochester, New York, who are opening a bed-and-breakfast in Friendship.

Sheila is under siege. But there are plenty of helping hands. One customer stacks the dirty dishes. Another pours the coffee. The New Yorkers take orders.

"She's out of the special today."

"Who has the ham and steak—I mean, ham and cheese??"

"That's a Pepsi you wanted with your steak sandwich? And coffee too?"

Watching the controlled chaos, you begin to figure out why they call this place Friendship.

The customers clear out, and calm returns to Sheila's Shanty. To a casual observer, it seems like Sheila has fed

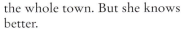
Vivian York, right, and her Lobster Lane Bookshop, above.

the whole town. But she knows better.

"No, not quite. The fishermen haven't been in yet . . . ."

At Chronicle, we know an exit line when we hear one. Peter and the Chevy hightail it out of Friendship.

Booking It

Driving along the coast of Maine, it is best not to be in a hurry. The geography of the place—all those coves and inlets—makes boat travel more direct than driving. Actually, the old Chevy steers like a boat, but it's still running like a top as it pulls into the village of Sprucehead.

Sprucehead is home to Vivian York and her Lobster Lane Bookshop. The shop is perched on a point above Penobscot Bay. Jammed inside its walls are upwards of 50,000 second-hand books—enough material to occupy a lifetime of Maine winters.

Vivian has a round, friendly face and is happy to guide visitors through the narrow aisles, pointing out books as she goes.

"This is the Maine section. And when you go through here, this gets you into the fiction. Here's juvenile. And poetry."

Vivian is the widow of a Sprucehead lobsterman. Don York, like his wife, was a great reader, and that led to them opening the store. "My husband felt that we needed something that he was able to work at in the wintertime," Vivian explains. "To stay away from the ice and the frozen ropes. Fishing gets pretty bad in the wintertime."

In between lobstering and the bookshop, Vivian and Don raised two sons and two daughters. Don passed away in 1974. Vivian has been running the shop herself ever since. Some people find it an unusual business for a town like Sprucehead. "Hodding Carter was in here one day and he said, 'This is a funny place to have a bookshop— it's a dead end. It's nowhere. Why have a shop up here?'" she recalls. "Well," I told him, "we live here! And he said, 'That's a good reason.'"

Vivian will sell you a hardcover book for just a few dollars and when you are done with it, she'll buy it back at half of what you paid for it. Between these creaky walls, you will find a variety of reading that would put most upscale bookstores to shame.

Jan Derry of Montana, above, and master builder, Dave Foster, center.

The Lobster Lane Bookshop has been delighting visitors for 23 years. But its long-term future is in doubt. "My children are not interested in it," Vivian sighs. "Unfortunately, when I am through with it, it is going."

Builders in Training

Heading north out of Sprucehead, a storm is brewing and the sea is rising. Rising too is the temperature gauge on the old Chevy, but it's nothing a little antifreeze doesn't cure. Soon, all is well again, and the Chevy is bound for Rockport, about 12 miles up the coast.

Down a narrow lane near the harbor sits the Rockport Apprentice Shop. Here, they teach boatbuilding—along with some other lessons. On this day, 14 young apprentices and four young interns are at work on a variety of traditional wooden boats. Apprentices put in two years here, receiving no pay. The shop calls its program "labor for learning."

Inside the workshop, wood chips and shavings are everywhere. Their scent fills the air. Bearded master builder Dave Foster leans across the stern of an unfinished boat.

"Make sure that board's parallel with this one," he reminds an apprentice.

Boats take shape under the tutelage of Foster and a journeyman. As he explains it, skills are absorbed mostly through osmosis. "They are pretty much on their own. Pretty much self-motivated. Actually, we're here just to help them out when they run into problems," he says. "A lot of the guys that have been here the longest will help them out. They'll pass on what they know."

The Apprentice Shop builds its boats to order, and Foster and his crew are fighting a deadline today. They are working on a 32-foot ketch, modeled after the boats that once carried fish from weirs in Passamoquoddy Bay to the sardine canneries in Eastport.

In an adjacent shop, smaller boats are being built. The young men here are interns—volunteers who might continue on as apprentices. They come from all over the world for the training. In the shop today is a German, an Italian, an Englishman, and a Bostonian.

This is hard, physical work. It is also a form of art. Most who come here will go on to find jobs in related fields. Others, like Jan Derry of Montana, will return to

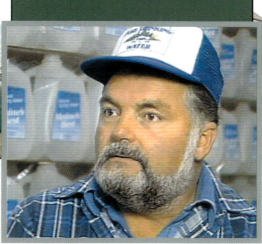

John Lohnes, center. Maybe Peter should be using "Maine's Best" in the Chevy's radiator . . .

prior jobs with a new outlook. "Much of what drew me here were the shapes, the lines. Before I got here, I built houses and cabinetry. Everything was straight and ninety degrees and flat." Derry says. "These things—they're alive, basically. Once you put them in the water and they launch, they have a whole new identity. It's like giving birth."

All Bottled Up

The Chevy heads west on Route 17, south of Camden Hills, toward the little town of Union. We want to find out whether John Lohnes is on the level. Word is he is bottling his well water and selling it for cash money.

John is a big strapping fellow with a dry Maine wit. He runs a general store in Union, and enjoys bantering with his customers.

It seems that the well water bubbling up from his land is some of the best tasting around. Two years ago, John had a brainstorm.

"We knew the water was good, and when people started coming over and filling their gallon jugs and bring-ing them home—and these are *local* people whose water isn't all that bad—well, I think to myself, we ought to have the big test to see what it actually is," John explains. "And the test comes back—'Pure,' it says. I think it is the purest water you can find anywhere. And so I just thought there would be a market out there for that type of water."

John calls his water "Maine's Best." He bottles it in a small plant that he built behind his general store. His is a family operation; his wife and daughter make up half the workforce.

Like most native Mainers, John has a sense of per-spective. He doesn't want to see "Maine's Best" grow too big. "I'm not interested in making a killing," he claims. "We're fortunate enough that we don't need a lot of money. But I'd like to make a living out of it, and I think we can do that without getting real big."

When asked if his water is really the best is Maine, John is quick to reply. "Without a doubt," he confirms. "Not only Maine's best. We could probably change the label to 'New England's Best.' Maybe 'Nation's Best!'" John adds, conceding that modesty has always been one of his virtues.

BOSTON HARBOR HAVENS

In 1988, the senior George Bush used the polluted state of Boston Harbor as a campaign weapon against then Massachusetts Governor Michael Dukakis. But, even as the political fight raged, the battle to clean up the harbor was already reaping dividends. In 1996, Washington recognized that progress by designating the area The Boston Harbor Islands National Recreation Area. Chronicle explored this forgotten treasure in the autumn of 1992, finding military history and an underused recreational resource.

From space, they appear like jewels at the mouth of Boston Harbor: 30 islands situated within the Greater Boston shoreline, with evocative names like Hangman, Raccoon, The Graves, Snake, and World's End. Some are rocky, barren places. Others are forested and lush. Many appear deserted, abandoned just miles from a major metropolitan area. But slowly they've come back to life as a recreational resource. That's no surprise, since as Stephen Carpenter, director of forests and parks for Massachusetts, points out: "You can be on a deserted island and look out across the bay and see skyscrapers. That's a tremendous combination. You can have the best of both worlds right here in your backyard."

Six islands—Bumpkin, Gallop's, George's, Grape, Lovell's, and Peddock's—are accessible to the public by ferry or water taxi. During the summer season, the islands are open daily from 9:00 A.M. until sunset; in spring and fall they're open only on weekends.

But according to Visitors Services Supervisor Eleanor Yahrmarkt, fear keeps many landlubbers from checking out their communal waterfront property. "People are always afraid of being abandoned on an island," Yahrmarkt says. "But there are island managers who live there 24 hours a day, and they always let you know when the boat is coming and going. So you're not going to miss the boat, and you're not going to not get home for dinner."

Yahrmarkt adds, "We don't have muggers out here and we don't have people looking for turf. It's all equal and everybody can enjoy themselves and have a good time."

Civil War Outpost

George's Island is the first site for arriving boats. Fort Warren is the first sight passengers see. Built between 1833 and 1869, Fort Warren was situated on George's Island because of its strategic location, close to two major shipping channels for Boston Harbor. During the Civil War, it was used first for training Union soldiers, and then became a camp for Confederate prisoners. Park Ranger Jonathan

Kranz researched its history.

"Fort Warren goes on record as being among the most humane of all prisoner-of-war camps during the Civil War," Kranz says. "Of about 1,200 people held here, only 13 died and those men died of natural causes."

Kranz says Fort Warren housed some prominent captives. "The most famous prisoner held here was Alexander Hamilton Stevens, who was the vice president of the Confederacy. He was captured at the end of the war, after Appomattox, and he stayed here for about six months."

On the first weekend of every August, Civil War history comes back to life, as Union and Confederate re-enactors gather for an encampment. Using a bit of dramatic license, they stage a battle that never really happened, with the public looking on free of charge.

Island Home

At 188 acres, Peddock's Island is the third largest in the chain; it is also one of the few that can be called inhabited, with a couple of year-round residents, and a sizeable contingent in summer. These "cottagers" have come for generations, owners of the structures they've built, but not the land the homes sit upon. They accepted living without

electricity or running water in return for some of the best views in town. Bob Enos's grandfather bought what was an old fishing shack at the turn of the last century.

"They always knew that all they owned was their cottage and that they had no rights to the land under the cottage," Enos says. "Still, you live with the belief that what is, is always going to be."

But in 1992, the cottagers faced an end to their idyllic summers. The Metropolitan District Commission, a Massachusetts agency that manages the island, threatened evictions because of environmental violations and the posting of illegal "private property" signs. A compromise was reached, under which the rustic tradition will continue only for the life of the present leaseholders. Then, the island will become totally public.

On the east end of the island there stands an abandoned military site, Fort Andrews. Today vandals attack it during unguarded times, leaving broken windows behind. But during World War II, it was 12-inch mortar practice that did the damage, says the MDC's Matt Tobin.

"They realized they had a real problem: the windows were breaking out of the buildings," Tobin explains. "The concussion from the firing of the mortars was so

heavy that it would blow the windows out."

Italian POWs were incarcerated on Peddock's during the war. According to a *Boston Globe* report, the prisoners seldom tried to escape, and so were rewarded with shopping trips to the city's North End.

Peddock's also lays claim to some prehistoric history. In the late 1960s, a summer resident digging in her garden found a male skeleton that carbon dating established to be 4,100 years old, the oldest human skeleton ever found in New England.

Lovell's Island is named after an early settler of Dorchester. It also had a military presence, Fort Standish, with remnants left today. It has a supervised swimming beach and a romantic landmark—the heart-shaped Lovers' Rock.

Bumpkin Island was donated to Harvard College in 1682. Tenant farmers worked its land until the 20th century; the foundation of a farmhouse from about 1800 is still there. A hospital for paraplegic children was built around 1900, but fire destroyed it in 1945. The Navy built barracks and other facilities during World War I; those were taken down after the war. In all, island manager Anne Conklin told us, there were 56 structures on

Bumpkin, and all were abandoned until the new park was created.

Isolation Island

Some islands will be reborn by the National Park designation. Spectacle Island is a prime candidate for resurrection. It's been home to a quarantine hospital, a horse rendering plant, and a grease extraction facility. For a time it tasted glory as a summer resort with two hotels, but for most of the last 50 years, it was a dump—literally. The city of Boston dumped garbage here, in some places up to 100 feet deep. More recently, it's taken fill from Boston's "Big Dig" highway and tunnel project.

Spectacle got its name because it looked like a pair of eyeglasses at low tide. Planners looking into its future hope to transform a once lowly trash heap into the highest island in the harbor, complete with a park, marina, visitor's center, and swimming beaches.

The Brewster Islands are also closed to the public. But unlike Spectacle, made inaccessible by humans, it is nature that's most responsible for the Brewsters' isolation. "The outer islands are in themselves a fort," explains Al Kenney, supervisor of the Boston Harbor Islands State Park. "They're high sheer cliffs of rock and very difficult to get aboard."

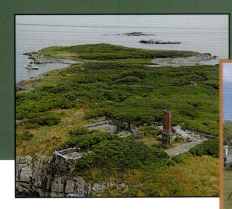

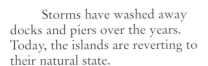

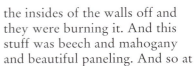

Storms have washed away docks and piers over the years. Today, the islands are reverting to their natural state.

Little Brewster Island is home to Boston Light. This was the first lighthouse built in the United States, in 1716, and the last to remain staffed, although not without a fight. The Coast Guard had planned to make it automated, like every other lighthouse it operated. But preservation groups and Senator Edward Kennedy prevailed in having Boston Light remain staffed by Coast Guard personnel.

Island Life Cycle

The story heard over and over on many of these islands is one of heavy use in Boston's early years—for fishing, farming, even industrial purposes—followed by military use by the Army and Navy, then finally neglect. Tiny Calf Island, just 17 acres, illustrates the pattern in microcosm. In 1902, stage and screen actress Julia Arthur and her husband built a mansion, "The Moorings," high on a cliff. Decades later, the Navy occupied it, and, according to Al Kenney, didn't prove to be the best caretakers.

"They had a severe winter one year and they ran out of heating material," Kenney explains. "So they tore the insides of the walls off and they were burning it. And this stuff was beech and mahogany and beautiful paneling. And so at the end, there was just the outer structure of the house." Vandals finished off what was left. Just one chimney out of five remains from the original grand home.

The group Friends of the Boston Harbor Islands deserves major credit for the rediscovery of Boston's forgotten treasures. Formed in 1979, the organization runs tours and educational programs, and advocates for responsible public use of the islands. The FBHI Web site (www.fbhi.org) is a font of information for anyone wanting to know more about each of the islands.

UPDATE: What is the future for the islands in Boston's Harbor? There are many proposals, including a marina on Spectacle Island, perhaps with a marine mammal rescue center, a family resort on Peddock's Island where Fort Andrews once stood, and a conference center on Boston-owned Long Island. The various city, state, and federal agencies that manage the islands are weighing the options.

MONHEGAN ISLAND

Monhegan Island is "a rock with a little bit of dirt thrown on it," according to one longtime resident. Just several miles off the Maine coast, it's worlds removed from a society that counts on malls and movie theaters for entertainment. In the summer of 1995, when Chronicle visited, electricity was still a novelty for some.

Island historians say Captain John Smith came to Monhegan looking for cod before he traveled on to Plymouth. In any event, fishing remains one of the major ways to make a living here, although it gets harder every year. Many residents go lobstering January to June, then fish for tuna in the summer.

But the major boat to look for from May to September is the ferry from the mainland. The 12-mile trip brings in the summer people, families who have come here for generations. They return to spend some time in a place that prizes simplicity, serenity, and solitude—a last vestige of Wild America.

Don't expect to find Wired America. Even though it was Theodore Edison, son of the inventor, who in 1954 helped organize Monhegan Associates to preserve the island's natural beauty, 24-hour electricity didn't come to The Island Inn, its largest bed and breakfast, until 1970.

Today, some cabin owners still make do without power, relying on kerosene lamps instead.

Making do is a required skill in a place like Monhegan. The year-round population is less than 100 people. Locals like Luke Church learn to occupy multiple professions: at the time of Chronicle's visit, he was simultaneously an island paramedic, health officer, road commissioner, backhoe operator, plumber, electrician, carpenter, and in charge of feeding the deer imported to Monhegan in the 1950s. (That last job no longer exists. Because of fears of Lyme disease, the island voted to eradicate the deer beginning in 1998.)

Artist Mile

Barely a square mile, Monhegan boasts dramatic 160-foot cliffs. Surreal sunsets. Some 600 species of wildflowers. It sometimes seems as though the same number of artists

*Sonya Sklaroff, above, and
Luke Church, far right.*

cover the island, especially from May to October, hoping to capture that beauty on canvas. Robert Henri, George Bellows, Edward Hopper, Andrew and Jamie Wyeth, and Rockwell Kent are some of the artists who've memorialized Monhegan. Artist Sonya Sklaroff says the island presents a unique problem: it is too picturesque, almost paralyzing a painter with choices.

This little island even has its own littler island: Manana. Manana was home to Maine's most celebrated hermit—Ray Phillips—who died in the late seventies, leaving behind the driftwood shacks he built. The island was also the site of a now-abandoned Coast Guard station, and is covered with rocks that some islanders say bear Viking inscriptions.

Monhegan is a hiker's paradise, with 17 miles of footpaths. If you take a walk through Cathedral Woods, named for its tall trees, be sure to look down as well. Some say that there are little gnomes living there, and if you pay attention, you can see the little stick homes built for them by kind Monhegans.

Getting There:

Monhegan is about a one-hour ferry ride from Port Clyde, Maine (www.monheganboat.com/; 207–372–8848) or New Harbor, Maine (www.hardyboat.com/monhegan.html; 800–278–3346).

CREDITS

PEOPLE

Grange Society, Original Air Date: May 1, 1992, Producer, Videographer, Editor: Art Donahue. *Story of a Storyteller,* Original Air Date: February 2, 1996, Producer, Videographer, Editor: Art Donahue. *Sting Operation,* Original Air Date: April 30, 1993, Producer: Roger Maroni; Videographer: Ken Sullivan; Editor: Jayne Raphael. *Cape Ann Artists,* Original Air Date: May 13, 1997, Producer: Lisa Pierpont; Videographers: Judi Guild, Art Egerton; Editors: Ron Sapp, Jayne Raphael, Debbie Therrien, Joe Mozdiez. *The Nut Lady,* Original Air Dates: November 20, 1984 and May 12, 1995, Producers: Lorie Conway, Joe Mozdiez; Videographers: David Skillicorn, Ken Sullivan; Audio: Doug Dike; Editors: Marcy Tankersley, Kathleen McKenna, Curt Reichenbach, Joe Mozdiez. *Mental Magellans,* Original Air Date: November 5, 1992, Producer: Clint Conley; Videographer: David Skillicorn; Editor: Joe Mozdiez. *The Knackerman,* Original Air Date: September 27, 1989, Producer: Rita Thompson; Videographer: Art Donahue; Audio: Bob Hakkila; Editors: Alan Pratt, Curt Reichenbach. *The Milkman,* Original Air Date: January 30, 1986, Producer: Lorie Conway. *Horse Sense,* Original Air Date: April 25 1990, Producer: Lynne McCrea; Videographer: Art Donahue; Audio: Bob Hakkila; Editor: Alan Pratt. *Portraits of the Past,* Original Air Date: July 6, 1992, Producer, Videographer, Editor: David Skillicorn

PLACES

Winnipesaukee Winter, Original Air Date: March 4, 1991, Producer: Clint Conley; Videographer: John Rosenfeld; Audio: John Mitchell; Editors: Susan Krieger, Leroy McLaurin, Curt Reichenbach. *Woodbury: Where New England Begins,* Original Air Date: August 4, 1992, Producer: Stella Gould; Videographers: Bob Oliver, Frank Konesky; Editor: Kathy McKenna. *The Mount Washington Hotel,* Original Air Dates: July 21, 1992, and February 16, 2000, Producers: Amy Shea, Ted Reinstein; Videographers: David Skillicorn, Ken Sullivan, Bob Oliver; Editors: Joe Mozdiez, Ellen Boyce. *Life on Sebago Lake,* Original Air Date: October 2, 2000, Producer, Videographer, Editor: Art Donahue. *The Berkshires' Gilded Age,* Original Air Date: May 23, 1989, Producer: Stella Gould; Videographer: Art Donahue; Audio: Bob Hakkila; Editors: Kurt Reichenbach, Ron Sapp. *Wandering Through Wiscasset,* Original Air Date: November 28, 1995, Producer: Amy Shea; Videographer: Bob Oliver; Editors: Joe Mozdiez, Jayne Raphael. *The Magic of Mount Kearsage,* Original Air Date: November 16, 1993, Producer: Karen Coker; Videographer: David Skillicorn, Editor: Debbie Therrien. *Swift River Valley,* Original Air Date: July 21, 1986, Producer: Bob Geballe; Videographer: David Skillicorn; Audio: Jim Fripp; Editors: Marcy Tankersley, David Teixeira. *Down East Determination,* Original Air Date: February 5, 1999, Producer: Myles Gordon; Videographer: Art Donahue; Editors: Joe Mozdiez, Jayne Raphael, Ron Sapp. *The Ultimate Flea Market,* Original Air Date: October 13, 1997, Producer: Clint Conley; Videographer: Art Donahue; Editor: Ron Sapp. *Islanders Wanted,* Original Air Date: February 10, 1987, Producer: Rita J. Thompson; Videographer: Alice Daly; Audio: Jim Fripp; Editors: Kathy McKenna, Curt Reichenbach. *The Real Golden Pond,* Original Air Dates: May 23, 1985, and July 26, 1995, Producers: Lorie Conway, Dick Amaral; Videographers: Judi Guild, Ken Sullivan; Audio: Jim Fripp; Editors: Jeff Brawer, Kathy McKenna.

ONLY IN NEW ENGLAND

For the Love of Lobsters, Original Air Date: July 14, 1992, Producer: Stan

Leven; Videographers: Art Donahue, Judi Guild; Editors: Joe Mozdiez, Mary Driscoll. *Abandoned New England,* Original Air Date: February 4, 1991, Producer, Videographer, Editor: Art Donahue. *Summer Camps for Grownups,* Original Air Date: July 25, 1994, Producer: Clint Conley; Videographers: Lance Douglas, David Skillicorn; Editors: Jayne Raphael, Nina Lee. *Quirky Collections,* Original Air Date: May 12, 1995, Producer: Joe Mozdiez; Videographer: Ken Sullivan; Editor: Joe Mozdiez. *The Mill River Disaster,* Original Air Date: May 6, 1993, Photographer, Producer, Editor: Art Donahue. *Out There,* Original Air Date: May 10, 1999, Producer: Clint Conley; Videographer: Carl Vieira; Editor: Ron Sapp. *A Harvest to Remember,* Original Air Date: November 22, 1995, Producer, Videographer, Editor: David Skillicorn. *All-American Three-Deckers,* Original Air Date: January 8, 2001, Producer: Stella Gould; Videographers: Judi Guild, Kevin Tierney, Bob Oliver; Editors: Ron Sapp, Joe Mozdiez. *Filling in the Gaps,* Original Air Date: November 30, 1994, Producer: Clint Conley; Videographer: David Skillicorn; Editor: Joe Mozdiez. *New England's Strangest Stories,* Original Air Date: May 5, 1995, Producer, Videographer, Editor: Art Donahue.

Haunting Local Legends, Original Air Date: October 31, 1996, Producer, Videographer, Editor: Art Donahue. *Sugar High,* Original Air Date: March 26, 1999, Producer: Stacy Lundin; Videographer: Judi Guild; Editor: Joe Mozdiez. *Roadside Curiosities,* Original Air Date: November 4, 1999, Producer: Stan Leven; Videographers: Carl Vieira, Judi Guild; Editors: Karen Lippert, Ron Sapp. *Circus Fire Tragedy,* Original Air Date: February 18, 2000, Producer, Videographer, Editor: Art Donahue. *Autumn Splendor,* Original Air Date: November 6, 2000, Producer, Videographer, Editor: Art Donahue.

ISLANDS & BYWAYS

Vermont's Snow Route, Original Air Date: March 4, 1998, Producer: Amy Shea; Videographer: Art Donahue; Editor: Joe Mozdiez. *Washed Ashore on Block Island,* Original Air Dates: July 26, 1989, and May 9, 1995, Producer: Lorie George; Videographer: Clayton Sizemore; Audio: Jim Fripp; Editors: Kathy McKenna, Alan Pratt, Ron Sapp; Producer: Clint Conley; Videographer: David Skillicorn; Editor: Brian Menz. *Mohawk Trail,* Original Air Date: November 23, 1994, Producer, Videographer, Editor: Art Donahue. *Vineyard Hospitality,* Original Air

Dates: November 14, 1984, September 11, 1989, November 13, 1998, May 16, 2000, Producer: Kathy Bickimer; Videographer: Judi Guild; Audio: Jim Fripp; Editor: Jeff Brawer; Producer: Pat Bates; Videographer: David Skillicorn; Audio: Jim Fripp; Editor: Kathy McKenna; Producer: Roger Maroni; Videographer: Carl Vieira; Editor: Joe Mozdiez; Producer: John Budris; Videographer: Kevin Tierney; Editor: Joe Mozdiez. *Old King's Highway,* Original Air Date: July 26, 1993, Producer: Lynne McCrea; Videographer: Judi Guild; Editor: Ellen Boyce. *Mount Desert Island,* Original Air Date: November 22, 1996, Producer: Roger Maroni; Videographer: Judi Guild; Editors: Joe Mozdiez, Ron Sapp, Jayne Raphael. *Along the Molly Stark Trail,* Original Air Date: March 3, 1999, Producer: Clint Conley; Videographer, Editor: George Ellard. *The Original "On the Road,"* Original Air Date: January 26, 1987, Producers: Peter Mehegan, Stan Leven; Videographer: Dick Dunham; Audio: Doug Dike; Editors: Kathy McKenna, Dave Teixeira, Joe Mozdiez. *Boston Harbor Havens,* Original Air Date: September 21, 1992, Producer, Videographer, Editor: Art Donahue. *Monhegan Island,* Original Air Date: July 19, 1995, Producer, Videographer, Editor: Art Donahue.

WCVB-TV EMPLOYEES

Our appreciation to all the WCVB-TV employees who have contributed their talents to Chronicle over the years:

Anchors and Reporters:
Peter Mehegan
Mary Richardson
Ted Reinstein
Mike Barnicle
Liz Brunner
Andria Hall
Chet Curtis
Donna Downs
Jeanne Blake
Arnie Reisman
Chuck Kraemer

Editorial
Chris Stirling
Susan Sloane
Mark Mills
Judy Stoia
Charlie Kravetz
Phil Balboni
Paul La Camera

Administrative
Leona McCarthy
Marilyn Garrett
Steve Lacy
Stacy Lundin
Kristin Reilly
Georgia Pappas
Rich Mello

Directors
Gregg Kidd
Bob Comiskey
Dave Lawless
Bill Lowell
Alyson Pressley
Phil Rubin
Dick Puttkamer

Engineering
Gerri Powers
Jack Barry

Control Room
Rob Crowley
Kim Devolve
Doug Devitt
Mary Driscoll
Bruce Goldman

Isaac Laughinghouse
Emmons S. Levine
George Nahas
Phil Walters

Producers
Dick Amaral
Kathy Bickimer
Clint Conley
Kathryn Farrelly
Myles Gordon
Stella Gould
Stan Leven
Lisa Pierpont
Amy Shea
Roger Maroni
Ramsey Trussell
Alison Mosher
Lisa Ziegler
Lisa Grace
Gonca Sonmez-Poole
Lorie Conway
Pat Bates
Rita Thompson
Jerry Kirschenbaum
Lisa Schmid
Bob Geballe
Lynne McCrea
Anne Albright
Betsey Arledge
Ron Blau
Vince Canzoneri
Joyce Ferriabough
Hamilton Fisher
Karen Holmes Ward
Tony Hill
Jo LaCour
Karl Nurse
Rory O'Connor
Kate Raisz
Debbie Pettibone
Caron Shapiro
Philis Shipman
Susan Sprecher

Editors
Joe Mozdiez
Jayne Raphael
Ron Sapp

Brian Menz
Ellen Boyce
Debbie Therrien
Jeff Brawer
Lisa Borge
Susan Krieger
Andi Clark
Curt Reichenbach
Nancy Maloney
Bob Marsocci
Kathy McKenna
Alan Pratt
Ted Phillips
Gretchen Soehner
Geoff Sullivan
Marcy Tankersley
Dave Teixeira
Bonnie Watson
Kathy Wilcox

Videographers
Judi Guild
Art Donahue
Bob Oliver
Carl Vieira
David Skillicorn
Ken Sullivan
Kevin Tierney
Steve Colvin
Alice Daly
Ed Dadulak
Dick Dunham
Rodney Grace
John Graham
Bill Hartigan
Cal Hoyle
Bob King
Chris O'Hare
John Rosenfeld
Howie Rouse

Field Audio
Doug Dike
Jim Fripp
Bob Hakkila
Jim Watson

FLEETING FOOTAGE

Six small New England states provide Chronicle's crews with an endless variety of stories, set among the mountains, valleys, rivers, lakes, and coastline in all four seasons. But the scenes we videotape appear only on your television for a few seconds. Unlike a single photograph you can look at and study, Chronicle tells stories with hundreds of images in each show, most never to be seen again. In addition, until recently our television cameras have limited us to a picture resolution of 480 lines—the broadcast standard we've all lived with since the 1940s. That began to change in November of 1998, when WCVB-TV, Channel 5, became the first station in New England to also broadcast digitally, on WCVB-DT, Channel 20. Digital transmission has opened the door for high definition television and on March 3, 1999, Chronicle made history with "The Molly Stark Trail," the first New England program shot and aired in high definition television. Videotaped with a picture resolution of 1,080 lines, the quality is stunning. The pages of this book contain both standard and high definition images taken from Chronicle stories over the years, as we've witnessed the nature of New England at its best.

Art Donahue
Editor/Videographer/Photographer